Buying a property in
MOROCCO

Other Living and Working Abroad titles
from How To Books

Live and Work in Turkey

France: A Handbook for New Residents

Live and Work in Brazil

Live and Work in France

Live and Work in Greece

howtobooks

For full details, please send for a free copy of the
latest catalogue to:
How To Books
Spring Hill House, Spring Hill Road, Begbroke
Oxford OX5 1RX, United Kingdom
info@howtobooks.co.uk
www.howtobooks.co.uk

Buying a property in

MOROCCO

Your essential
guide to
purchasing,
letting, selling
and living in
the world's
hottest new
destination

LEAONNE HALL

howtobooks

Published by How To Books Ltd,
Spring Hill House, Spring Hill Road,
Begbroke, Oxford OX5 1RX, United Kingdom.
Tel: (01865) 375794. Fax: (01865) 379162.
info@howtobooks.co.uk
www.howtobooks.co.uk

How To Books greatly reduce the carbon footprint of their books by
sourcing their typesetting and printing in the UK.

British Library Cataloguing in Publication Data
A catalogue record for this book is available from the British Library

ISBN 978 1 84528 265 3

Cover design by Baseline Arts Ltd, Oxford
Produced for How To Books by Deer Park Productions, Tavistock, Devon
Typeset by TW Typesetting, Plymouth, Devon
Printed and bound by Cromwell Press, Trowbridge, Wiltshire

NOTE: The material contained in this book is set out in good faith for
general guidance and no liability can be accepted for loss or expense incurred
as a result of relying in particular circumstances on statements made in the
book. The laws and regulations are complex and liable to change, and
readers should check the current position with the relevant authorities before
making personal arrangements.

Contents

Acknowledgements

My thanks go to Mark Wheatley for all his help and support throughout this project. I would also like to thank Loïc Raboteau and the team at The International Property Law Centre, and Matthew Weston and the team at Blevins Frank for all the information and help they supplied. Thanks also go to Frances McKay at estate agents Francophiles, Adam Cornwell of GEM Estates, Peter Weedon and Steve Burns of Compass Properties, and to Sarah Chambers of holiday-rentals.co.uk. Heartfelt thanks also go to Nathalie Roberts for checking my school-girl French!

Preface

Morocco is an exotic, diverse and exciting country – a taste of Africa on the edge of Europe. This is a colourful, welcoming place that really excites the senses, from the bustling souks and ancient medinas to the sandy dunes and desolate expanses of the Sahara. The fascinating nature of this country is just one of the reasons why it has become such an appealing destination for home buyers.

What makes Morocco so interesting from an investment point of view is the forward-thinking approach of its king, Mohammed VI, who is keen to turn the country into a major global force. Taking a similar approach to Dubai in terms of revitalising its economy and tourism industry, this is an exciting time for the previously overlooked African nation. Morocco has grown in leaps and bounds and is now successfully attracting international investment, both in the form of home buyers and developers. Yet this isn't unchecked development – thankfully, Morocco is being incredibly careful with its dynamic expansion, keeping apartment block and development heights to a minimum and enforcing strict planning rules within the medinas, ensuring that the fascinating culture and diversity of traditions that exist here continue to thrive.

As the world becomes an increasingly small place, with cheap flights taking us around the globe, hidden markets such as Marrakesh have hit the investment radar, and thanks to the small price tags and beautiful, traditional homes for sale, people are keen to secure their own piece of Moroccan real estate. However, I would urge anyone thinking of buying here to take the time to really embrace the

Moroccan culture and lifestyle as this is the only way you will get a real insight into the essence of this country.

This is a great time to buy in Morocco, and this book should help you to find your ideal home. Just remember, research is the key to a successful and pain-free purchasing process!

Good luck,
Leaonne Hall

Note

Throughout this book I have attempted to be as accurate as possible with every fact and figure used. The pound–dirham exchange rate at the time of writing was £1 = 16.2020 dirhams, but as these rates fluctuate daily, you should always carry out exchange-rate checks of your own when looking at the Moroccan market. I have used 'dirhams' throughout; the abbreviations 'MAD' and 'DH' are also commonly used.

In reference to place names, in many instances there are a number of different ways to spell a town, city or village – for example, Fes, Fez or Fès, and Marrakesh or Marrakech. For the purposes of this book, I have used the English names.

Country fact file

Population: 33.7 million
Population growth rate: 1.528%
Capital City: Rabat
Area: Total: 446,550 sq km (Land: 446,300 sq km,
  Water: 250 sq km)
Government: Constitutional monarchy
Head of State: King Mohammed VI
GDP real growth rate: 9.4%
Inflation: 2.1%
Unemployment rate: 7.7%
Net migration: −0.82 migrant(s)/1,000 population
Currency: Moroccan dirham (MAD or DH)
Exchange rate: £1 = 16.2020 dirhams
Major trading partners: Spain, France, USA, UK
Time zone: UTC (GMT + 0, same as UK time)
Dialling code: + 212

1
Introduction to Morocco

BUYING ABROAD AND WHAT IT CAN OFFER

Morocco has recently arrived on the international property scene for a number of reasons. For starters it has a progressive forward thinking leader, a growing economy and excellent appreciation rates. Secondly, and most importantly for a number of potential re-locators, it enjoys a fabulous climate, miles of sandy white beaches, an unspoilt and diverse landscape, an exotic climate and a fascinating culture. No surprise then that Morocco has become a major target for investors, second-home buyers and permanent relocators looking for a better lifestyle.

Twenty years ago buying abroad was considered a difficult and risky business, but today perceptions have altered, and now more than one in ten Britons live overseas, with 400,000 owning a property abroad. Foreign currency exchange experts, HiFX, recently published figures which stated that the British equity in overseas property now stands at a staggering £52 billion, with an average of 500 Britons leaving UK shores every day to start a new life or take up a job overseas. In the last five years, the number of people buying overseas has risen by 60% from 129,000 in 2000/2001 to 211,000 in 2006.

It wasn't until the advent of the package holiday and the mass development of the Spanish property market in the 1970s and 1980s that the idea of owning a home in the sun became a popular option, soon developing into a feasible prospect as international estate

1

agents and mortgage lenders came on the scene. Today, thousands of us – 68% of British adults, that's 29 million people – want to buy a home abroad, and thanks to the increased freedom of movement courtesy of EU regulations (which allow us to move around with only the need for a passport rather than reams of paperwork), budget airlines and an opening of the overseas mortgage markets, this dream can now become a reality.

Once deterred by the cost, hassle and uncertainty of the overseas property market, people used to shy away from relocating and buying a home abroad, with this occupation being left to the rich or rootless. Today, property has become the cornerstone of our investment portfolio as we have seen our faith in the pensions and stock market undercut by the increasing volatility in the equity markets. What's more, as the British housing market has continued to boom, many buyers – especially first-time buyers – have been priced out of the UK market, but have seen their money go further, with greater returns, if buying abroad.

The lure of living abroad has traditionally been the desire for better weather and an improved and cheaper lifestyle. However, many have also begun to cite reasons such as rising crime, stealth taxes and political correctness gone wrong as reasons for leaving the UK and relocating their family overseas, and the figures show that long-term migration from Britain has hit an all-time high, reaching 385,000 from January to July 2006.

A new but significant trend has seen many people looking away from the traditional markets of Spain, France and Italy, and to the more emerging, new and culturally unspoilt markets, such as Morocco and many countries in Eastern Europe and South America. Keen to buy abroad in order to secure themselves a new and exciting lifestyle – as well as a nest egg for the future – buyers have become more adventurous, as investing the pound overseas has become a common, and relatively easy, occurrence. Eager to explore different cultures, away from the security of an expat development,

2

emerging markets such as Morocco have benefited from the desire people have to live a 'foreign' lifestyle and learn about new cultures, rather than choosing to place themselves smack in the middle of a 'Little Britain'.

Finally, there's the financial benefits to be reaped from buying overseas. Research by MRI Overseas Property suggests that six in ten Brits (63%) would now consider moving abroad, with 5% – one in 20 – of these considering moving for tax reasons. Most notably, nearly one in five (17%) of people considering buying a property abroad would purchase overseas purely as an investment for the future.

Many question the logic behind risking your hard-earned cash in an emerging market, when you can invest it 'safely' in the UK. However, the difference between buying in the 'safe' UK market and an emerging destination such as Morocco is the market growth and potential for higher returns from your investment. For example, UK capital growth currently sits at around 5%, meaning if you went out tomorrow and bought a property in the UK, hung on to it for one year and then sold it, your profit would be less than 10% of the property value. Compare this with the Moroccan market where annual appreciation rates regularly hit 20% to 30%, and it's easy to see which scenario offers the best investment potential. What's more, it has been reported that 2008 will see a stalling of the UK property market, and while this may be good news for those looking to climb onto the property ladder for the first time, for current homeowners it can be a worrying period.

WHY BUY IN MOROCCO?

Throughout the 1960s and 1970s Morocco was frequented by backpackers and was a favoured haunt of hippies. Today this has all changed. Morocco is becoming one of the fastest growing destinations among holidaymakers and overseas property buyers alike, attracting increasing numbers of visitors and rising levels of

3

investment into the country. Only three hours flight from the UK, Morocco has the advantage of being a more exotic location than nearby southern Spain, while it has a much more developed industry, economy and infrastructure than the African continent it belongs to. Economically, the country is being rapidly modernised thanks to forward-thinking monarch King Mohammed VI, who shares many of the aims and ambitions of Dubai's ruler Sheikh Mohammed bin Rashid Al Maktoum. If he's anywhere near as successful in his ambitions as that of Duabi's leader, then it is clear that Morocco has a big future. In 2001 King Mohammed unveiled his ambitious Plan Azur which aims to double tourist figures by 2010, construct 1,000 kilometres of new roads, introduce more budget flights through its Open Skies policy and expand the airports – and all of this equates to a €2.2 billion government investment. The most notable development for property buyers is the plan to create six new coastal resorts complete with residential properties and stacks of leisure facilities and amenities.

Thanks to the efforts of King Mohammed and his government, Morocco is on the verge of a property boom, with prices continuing to rise at levels of up to 50% in some areas. Despite these price hikes, property still remains incredibly affordable in UK terms, with housing retailing at one-third to a half that of Spanish and French levels. You can buy a ruined hovel for as little as £10,000 or an expansive villa for £300,000, making this an affordable country to buy in. However, if you're looking for something more luxurious, then there are also plenty of high-end properties.

There are no restrictions on foreigners buying in the country and in return for their investment, buyers benefit from a low cost of living and the rescinding of capital gains tax after ten years of ownership, as well as no inheritance tax.

The appeal of the country is obvious and this has helped to burgeon the blossoming tourism market and in turn impact positively upon investment prospects. Aside from being on the budget flight trail and within three hours of the UK, it has a mystique and mystery epitomised by its souks, mosques and medieval medinas, yet also boasts a modern, cosmopolitan side, highlighted by the metropolises of Marrakesh and Casablanca. Lush gardens, olive groves and palm trees contrast with the arid expanse of the western Sahara in the south, while the developing ski resorts of the central Atlas mountains are only a couple of hours from the western coastline and its beaches. Year-round sunshine, purpose-built tourist facilities and some wonderful beaches all combine to make this the ultimate tourist destination, with Morocco's Mediterranean coast stretching for 450 km and its Atlantic Coast – which has some of the best surfing and windsurfing conditions in the world – for 3,000 km. Politically, the country remains stable and the economy is blossoming, experiencing growth of around 6.7%. With such a positive future ahead of it, it is unsurprising that Morocco has become such a popular location for holidaymakers and buyers alike.

Insider info

Adam Cornwell, Managing Director of GEM Estates, takes a look at the popularity of Morocco and what it can offer investors.

Morocco is exceedingly popular with the Brits – just pick up any of the lifestyle, travel, women's interest or property magazines out there and you're bound to see some mention of it. GEM Estates initially began recommending and selling property in Morocco almost three years ago, but at that time it was just the die-hard Morocco fans who already knew and understood the country's charms. However, over the last three years we've seen Morocco's popularity grow, with the country beginning to appeal to a wide audience. All-purpose resorts such as Mediterrania Saïdia give people a balance of old and new Morocco and an easy introduction to life there, with golf courses, marinas and shopping malls all on site, and this has attracted a new breed of buyers. Meanwhile, investors, who may not necessarily be fans of Morocco but can see the obvious appeal of prices which are much lower than Spain, are also getting involved. What people also need to realise is that we're still at the thin end of wedge, with other Plan Azur resorts, EMAAR (Dubai developers) and Middle Eastern developers yet to start their projects, so ultimately prices are going to continue to rise.

Reasons to invest in Morocco

Property market	Lifestyle	Economy	Financial
◆ Prices are much lower than more established western resorts ◆ The property system is similar to the UK, with freehold and leasehold properties ◆ Your investment will be secure as there are a number of government-backed resorts being built ◆ Costal properties are offering an excellent investment as tourism in these areas increased by 18% among British tourists alone between 2004–2005 ◆ Appreciation rates are high at around 20%, with prices set to continue rising up to 2010	◆ Morocco offers a low cost of living and a luxurious lifestyle ◆ The African magic and mystique makes this a culturally interesting place to live ◆ There is year-round sunshine and this is an ideal winter sun location ◆ There are beautiful beaches, and a climate conducive to sunbathing and skiing ◆ Morocco is close to Europe and easy to reach from the UK, being on the budget flights route	◆ The increase in the tourist industry will result in demand for rental properties and excellent returns in the future – especially for golfing properties ◆ Morocco has a stable, forward-thinking government who are investing in the country ◆ The Open Skies policy means there are numerous budget airlines flying into Morocco and more are planned for 2008–2010	◆ There is no property gains tax to pay, and low capital gains tax ◆ You can secure a 60–70% mortgage ◆ Inheritance tax is non-existent ◆ There are no restrictions on foreign buyers

A BRIEF HISTORY OF MOROCCO

Morocco's Arabic name is Al-Maghrib Al-Aqsa, which means 'extreme west' and highlights Morocco's geographical and social position in the Arabic world. Shaped by the many cultures who have invaded and conquered the country over the years, Morocco has a long and illustrious history. Inhabited since Neolithic times, with evidence of occupation as far back as 15,000 BC, the earliest indigenous settlers were known as the Berbers, which literally means 'non-Arabs' or 'barbarians'. Split into various tribes, they lived – and in some cases still do live – in the inhospitable desert and mountain terrain of the country.

Part of the Maghreb – the name applied to the modern area of Morocco, Algeria, Tunisia and Libya – the origins of the country remain a mystery, as does that of the Berber tribes. In ancient times Morocco was developed by the Phoenicians, and later the Carthaginians, as a trading outpost, and the latter introduced a number of ports, towns and cities, with Tangiers being the most important. Consequently, when Carthage was sacked, Morocco became part of the Roman Empire, and following that civilisation's collapse, passed in quick succession to the Vandals, Visigoths, and then the Byzantine Greeks. Throughout this period, the Berbers held onto the mountainous, inhospitable lands of Morocco, which were simply regarded as hostile territory by the occupiers.

By the 7th century, following the death of the prophet Mohammed, the Islamic expansion began. The first Islamic attempt to occupy Morocco began in AD 669 but was quashed by the Berbers. However, towards the end of the 7th century, the Islamic invaders were more successful, and many Berbers converted to Islam. Nevertheless, the instilling of a new faith into the local populace backfired on the Islamic occupiers when the Berbers ousted them in the 8th century. This move marked the end of direct Arabic rule over Morocco.

7

The Berber dynasties

From the ousting of the Arab invaders, right through until the modern day, Morocco has been successfully ruled by a variety of Berber dynasties, starting with the **Idrissids** in the 8th century. This dynasty was founded by Moulay Idriss, a political exile from Mecca and a direct descendent of the prophet Mohammed. Eventually poisoned by one of his many enemies, he was succeeded by his son, Idriss II, who built Fès and turned it into the state capital. He was also responsible for transforming Morocco into the first Arab kingdom, introducing currency, administration and an army into the country's north. However, despite his many achievements he never managed to unite the whole country, and on his death, infighting among his sons tore the dynasty apart.

Next came the **Almoravids** in the 11th century, a military confederation of Berber tribes who united and ruled the south under a strict form of Islam. Known as 'the veiled ones' due to the turbans they wore to protect their faces from the sands of the Sahara, their reign only lasted for 85 years, with their legacy being the transformation of Marrakesh into the Almoravid capital.

In the mid 12th century, the Almoravids were overthrown by the fervent religious group the **Almohades** (meaning 'believers in the unity of God'), who were angered by the lax rule Morocco had fallen under. They set up a dynasty which became known as the golden age of the Maghreb. Wrenching control of Spain from the Christians, and Tunisia back from Norman hands, leader Yacoub al-Mansour introduced an age of cultural and economic resurgence. However, with their forces spread so thinly, this power was not to last, and the Almohades dynasty fell in the 13th century to the patriotic **Merenids**, who left a fine architectural legacy in Fès.

The 16th century saw Morocco split into two and ruled by two competing dynasties, the **Wattasids** in Fès, who usurped the Merenids, and the Arabic **Saadian** dynasty who were based in Marrakesh. The Saadians ultimately prevailed, bringing an end to the rule of the Moroccan Berbers and the start of the Arab dynasties, which remains to the present day.

The Berbers

There has been much mystery surrounding the origination of the Berber people, although we do know that the Berbers have lived in the North African area – between western Egypt and the Atlantic Ocean – for as long as written records have been kept in the region. The earliest references to the Berbers are found in Saharan cave art, and there have also been references to them in the writings of the ancient Egyptians, Greeks and Romans.

Morocco is home to the largest proportion of the Berbers, with nearly 19 million (30%) of the total population living there. Between 8% to 15% of Berbers live in Algeria, and many in France, Niger and Spain. Most are Sunni Muslims. There have been tensions between Moroccan Berbers and the government, much of which relates to the banning of Berber names being given to children – they must be Arabic.

Centuries of change

The 17th century saw Morocco fall into civil war as the Saadian succession was disputed and the **Alawites**, tribal descendents of Mohammed from Arabia, seized control. Their rule gave rise to Morocco's greatest tyrant, Moulay Ismael. While he returned peace and stability to the country, improving international relations, many lives were lost in the process. However, by breaking down the tribes and imposing centralised rule he created a stable Moroccan state. To this day, the ruling dynasty in the country are the Alawites.

During this period, Europe was re-emerging as a power to rival the Arab State, who had controlled much of the Iberian Peninsula for many years. France and Spain plotted to seize and divide up Morocco between themselves, and in March 1912, the Treaty of Fès was signed, leaving Morocco under control of a French Protectorate. While the French respected the Muslim faith of Morocco's people, they introduced a French way of life into the country, with French become the country's first language, and this influence remains to this day, particularly in many of the country's Ville

Nouveau (new towns) and architecture. While the infrastructure, education system and commerce were all improved under French rule, tensions against the French were evident and nationalistic tendencies rife. In 1955, after prolonged demands from the Moroccan people, the Sultan was reinstated, having been exiled in the 1940s, and this paved the way to independence in 1956, when the Sultan was recognised as both the King and Prime Minister.

Modern Morocco under Hassan II

Succeeding Mohammed V – the Sultan whose return heralded independence to Morocco – Hassan II was hugely influential in creating present-day Morocco. Ruling for four decades from 1961 to 1999, he introduced the constitution to the Moroccan people and declared the Kingdom a social, democratic and constitutional democracy. 1963 saw the first democratic elections held, and while the next two decades saw upheaval and riots, in 1972 a third constitution was approved in which the power of the monarch was strengthened, and more parliamentary representatives elected. During the Cold War and the first Iraq war, he sided with the West.

On his death, many feared a power struggle and political vacuum, but his son succeeded the throne smoothly. King Mohammed VI still rules today and has moved the country forward in leaps and bounds, improving health, education and infrastructure, as well as reducing poverty. The economy has strengthened, as have the country's relations with the West through encouraged foreign investment. Most radically, he introduced a new bill for women's rights, which saw women created as equal in the eyes of the law and granting them protection and rights in marriage, divorce and child custody. He has also focused his attentions on revamping the much-overlooked northern region.

With such a ruler at the helm, Morocco has become a forward-thinking state and a major power, with a Western outlook that sits comfortably alongside its Arabic heritage. As previously mentioned, Mohammed VI introduced the progressive Plan Azur which aims to turn Morocco into a tourist hotspot, revitalising and diversifying the previously flagging economy. At present, thanks to Plan Azur, Morocco is on course to become the next Dubai and a dynamic economic power.

POLITICS AND ECONOMY

Politically, Morocco is a constitutional monarchy ruled by Mohammed VI, and has been an independent state since 1956.

Economically, the country has experienced encouraging expansion, with the GDP growth rate rising from 4.4% in 2004 to 6.7% in 2006. The International Monetary Fund has described Morocco's economic transformation between 2006 and 2007 as 'remarkable', and it is thanks to its diversification policy that the country has achieved such success – the African Development Bank recently cited Morocco as the fifth largest economic power in Africa, accounting for 7% of the continent's entire GDP.

Thanks to Plan Azur, moves are being made to help significantly strengthen the blossoming economy. With King Mohammed VI aiming to increase the number of foreign visitors to the country to 10 million by 2010, there has been an expansion in building development, resulting in the construction of 80,000 new hotel rooms and the creation of 600,000 new jobs. This in turn has helped to more than quadruple tourism and foreign investment in Morocco. Consequently, tourism is expected to account for 20% of the country's GDP by 2010.

Also, with the infrastructure and accessibility – into and around the country – set to improve, increasing interest in Morocco is being shown by foreign investors and multinationals. For instance, UAE developer Emaar has pledged £3.5 billion in Moroccan property initiatives.

Morocco's currency (the dirham) has appreciated by 18% since 1990, and by 2010, Morocco aims to become part of the Euro-Med Free Trade zone, working towards a closer relationship with the EU. With the dirham pegged strongly to the euro, vast fluctuations and instability in the currency are unlikely.

Currently, the major problems faced by the country are unemployment in urban areas and poverty among the populous, both of which the government are taking measures to counteract, with the introduction of affordable housing being one of their proactive measures.

King Mohammed VI has stated that the country is working to achieve some of the following goals:

◆ The final settlement of tensions in the disputed southern territory of the Western Sahara

◆ A continuation of reforms leading to the transformation of Morocco into a fully democratic state

◆ The creation of a modern, competitive and productive economy which can compete in the global market place

◆ The boosting of Morocco's status as a regional and international player

◆ Improved training and education for the populous

◆ Reformation of cultural and religious insititutions

◆ Promotion of rural development and the agricultural sector

Insider info

Steve Burns, Marketing Manager of Compass Properties, explains the transformation of Morocco from an unknown country into a lucrative property and investment hotspot.

The biggest change in the last few years has been the emergence of Morocco as a fantastic place to invest and a viable destination for overseas property purchasers. This has been driven principally by the new King, featured recently in *Time* magazine as 'The Cool King' – a young man with pro-Western values, loved almost unanimously by the Moroccan people.

The King has proposed a plan known as Vision 2010 (or Plan Azur), which aims to attract 10 million tourists to the country per annum by 2010. This is already becoming a reality as tourist figures have jumped from 4.2 million to 7 million in the last few years. $10 billion is to be invested into the infrastructure, and the King's initiative has already led directly to huge improvement projects being undertaken, such as new roads, ports, railways and airport improvements. The motorway network is being expanded, with a new high-speed route cutting the journey time from Tangier to Tetouan to 45 minutes, and a new port is shortly due for completion north of Tangier, which will be one of the largest in the region. The port's industrial park and associated benefits – such as a free trade zone – are set to increase employment, which will in turn boost demand for property in the area.

Morocco has already embraced an Open Skies policy, encouraging flights from all over Europe, and easyJet now flies daily to Marrakesh, with further routes to be announced shortly, including an expected service to Tangier. Meanwhile Ryanair has signed a five-year deal to open up 20 new routes.

GEOGRAPHY AND POPULATION

Separated from Spain only by the 13 km stretch of the Straits of Gibraltar, part of which Morocco controls, the country is located on the crossroads between east and west. Situated on the northernmost tip of Africa, Morocco borders Algeria to the west, while the Canary Islands lie just off the eastern coast. Lapped to the east by the waters of the Atlantic Ocean, the Mediterranean Sea lies to the north, with Morocco's coastline stretching for over 1,000 miles. Four Spanish enclaves actually lie on Morocco's Mediterranean coast – those of Ceuta, Melilla, Peñón de Vélez de la Gomera and Peñón de Alhucemas, as well as the Chafarinas Islands.

The country can be clearly divided into four geographical zones. The first consists of the coastline, with the resorts and beaches that are found along the Mediterranean and Atlantic shores. Next are the peaks of the Atlas and Rif Mountains, followed by the interior plains, complete with the Imperial cities. Finally, you have the desert areas of the Sahara.

Running down the backbone of the country are the Atlas Mountains, while the Rif Mountains – an extension of the Atlas ranges – run from east to west, in the country's north. In total, Morocco covers 446,550 sq km of land, with arable land accounting for 18% of the country, and forest covering a further 12%, making this a surprisingly lush and verdant country.

The desert of the Western Sahara region covers an area of 266,000 sq km, and lies to the south of the country. This region is sparsely populated and poor, especially when compared with the rich coastal plains, where the majority of agriculture is focused. Over half of the population live in the region's one main city, El Aaiún (Laâyoune). This disputed territory was formerly a Spanish colony, but was claimed by Morocco in 1975. Currently, it is on the UN list of Non-Self-Governing Territories, and has been since the 1960s, with both the Moroccans and the Arabic Polisario Front independence movement claiming control of the region. Many Moroccans have strong feelings about the Western Sahara and see it as undoubtedly a part of Morocco. King Mohammed VI opposes any referendum on independence, and has said Morocco will never agree to one. He stated, 'We shall not give up one inch of our beloved Sahara, not a grain of its sand.'

The 16 regions of Morocco:

- Chaouia-Ouardigha
- Doukkala-Abda
- Fès-Boulemane
- Gharb-Chrarda-Béni Hssen
- Greater Casablanca
- Guelmim-Es Semara
- Laâyoune-Boujdour-Sakia El Hamra
- Marrakesh-Tensift-El Haouz
- Meknès-Tafilalet
- Oriental
- Oued Ed-Dahab-Lagouira

- ◆ Rabat-Salé-Zemmour-Zaer
- ◆ Souss-Massa-Draâ
- ◆ Tadla-Azilal
- ◆ Tangier-Tétouan
- ◆ Taza-Al Hoceima-Taounate

Morocco has a population of 33.7 million, and a growth rate of 1.528%. Rabat is the capital, with a population of 1.7 million, while Casablanca is Morocco's main port and also its largest city with 3.1 million people. Morocco is the fourth most populous Arab country after Egypt, Sudan and Algeria, and most of the population are Sunni Muslims of Arab, Berber, or mixed Arab-Berber descent. About three-quarters of all present-day Moroccans are of Berber descent, while Arabs form the second largest ethnic group: Arab-Berber 99.1%, other 0.7%, Jewish 0.2%.

Population of Morocco's urban areas
- ◆ Casablanca: 3.1 million
- ◆ Rabat: 1.7 million
- ◆ Marrakesh : 1 million
- ◆ Fès: 946,815
- ◆ Agadir: 678,596
- ◆ Tangier: 669,680
- ◆ Meknès: 536,322
- ◆ Essaouira: 69,493

CLIMATE

Morocco's climate varies depending on your location, with extreme temperatures and conditions found in parts, and a moderate and subtropical climate cooled by breezes from the Mediterranean Sea and Atlantic Ocean in other areas. The northern coastal region enjoys a Mediterranean climate, while the southern Sahara is unsurprisingly arid and dry. On the coast the weather tends to be mild, with temperatures varying from 12°C in winter up to 24°C during the summer months; this is an area prone to humidity and very strong winds.

In the desert, temperatures can soar to 30°C even during the winter months, while the nights are cold, with temperatures sometimes reaching freezing point.

In the mountainous inland areas it can get bitterly cold during winter. With peaks rising to 4,163 m at their highest point and snow-capped for most of the year, temperatures here can easily drop below zero. Snowfall can be very heavy during the winter months, hence the increasing popularity of the Atlas range with skiers. The winters in the north of the country are wet and rainy, while in the south, at the edge of the Sahara, it is generally dry and bitterly cold.

	Tangiers	Casablanca	Marrakesh	Fès
January	16/6.35	17/4.6	18/1.88	15/4.23
February	12/4.86	18/3.32	20/1.91	17/3.29
March	19/4.21	19/2.83	23/2.59	20/3.47
April	20/4.25	20/2.31	25/2.35	21/3.76
May	22/2.52	22/0.87	28/0.51	25/2.44
June	26/0.53	24/0.29	32/0.23	30/0.64
July	29/0.18	26/0.09	37/0.03	34/0.06
August	29/0.09	26/0.02	36/0.19	34/0.21
September	27/1.66	26/0.44	32/0.62	30/1.14
October	24/7.16	24/2.8	28/1.42	25/4
November	20/7.91	21/5.34	23/1.69	20/4.19
December	17/10.09	18/5.43	20/1.77	16/5.09

Average temperature in °C and precipitation in cm.

RELIGION

One of the first things that really grabs your attention in Morocco – and an aspect of life here that every traveller will always remember – is the five daily calls to prayer that ring out across every town and city seven days a week. Islam is Morocco's largest religion, with 98.7% of the population practising Muslims. It was first introduced to Morocco back in 670 AD during the second Arab invasion. Christianity represents a mere 1.1% of the population and Judaism just 0.2%.

Islam

Islam is the second largest religion in the world after Christianity and in Morocco it is the official religion, permeating every aspect of life and dictating everything from the way you dress to how you organise your day. A monotheistic religion – meaning a religion which only follows one god or deity – Islam originates from the teachings of the Arabic prophet Mohammad, a religious and political figure who lived in the 7th century. It is believed that Mohammed was God's final prophet and the teachings of Islam are based around his word and deed – Sunnah – along with the words of the Qur'an. The word Islam means 'submission', highlighting the need for the total surrender of your life to God.

Islam has many religious practises, but the main ones followed by Muslims are the Five Pillars of Islam. These are Shahadah, the profession of faith; Salah, ritual prayer; Zakah, the payment of alms tax; Sawm, fasting during Ramadan; and Hajj, or the pilgrimage to Mecca. Islam also has its own laws, the sharia, which govern all aspects of Muslim life. These cover everything from your diet and banking, to warfare and marriage, telling you how to act in all events.

Back in the 7th century, Muslims split into different factions, the Sunni and the Shia. Shias adhere to the teachings of Mohammad and the religious guidance of his family, following the eight pillars of Islam rather than five adopted by the Sunni. Sunnis generally accept the rule of the caliphate of Abu Bakr rather than those of Mohammed. Sunni is the more popular form of Islam, with approximately 85% of Muslims following these teachings – including Moroccans – while the remaining 15% are Shias.

17

LANGUAGE

Morocco's official language is classical Arabic, although most people also speak French and have a perplexing habit of blending languages together when using them – a rather relaxed approach is taken to grammar when speaking. French, while being unofficially the country's second language, is universally recognised as the language of government, commerce and economics and is widely taught. In the north, 20,000 Moroccans unsurprisingly speak Spanish as a second language, with English still behind French and Spanish in terms of usage and popularity. However, many young Moroccans are beginning to speak English and consequently it is being introduced in many schools. If you are looking to buy or move to Morocco, you would benefit from learning French, as it is easier to grasp than Arabic and is widely used.

The Moroccans love to talk, and it's not uncommon to find Moroccans who speak up to four languages, with many also speaking a Berber dialect as well as Arabic and Moroccan. The country's Arabic dialect is known as Moroccan Arabic, although roughly 12 million people – 40% of the population – speak one of three Berber dialects, either Tarifit, Tashelhiyt, or Tamazight.

> **Did you know?**
> Berber was not recognised as an official language until 2003, but it still has no alphabet or system of writing. Despite Berbers being Morocco's indigenous population, there are laws in place that restrict the usage of the Berber dialect and all children must be given Arabic names.

FOOD AND DRINK

As with many things in Morocco, the cuisine is hugely diverse and has a blend of international influences, which over the years have been moulded together to produce today's local foods and recipes. Influences range from Berber, Spanish, Corsican and Portuguese, to

Arabic, Middle Eastern, Mediterranean, Turkish and African, and all have helped to shape the local cuisine. As most people know, spices are central to Moroccan cooking, having been imported into the country for centuries, and the most commonly used include paprika, saffron, chilli powder, cumin, coriander, cinnamon, mint, ground ginger and cayenne pepper.

Traditional home cooking is still important in Morocco, and despite the increased western influence that has seeped into the country, cooking remains the domain of women, with recipes and dishes handed down from generation to generation; consequently, the concept of measurements is fairly non-existent.

Meal times play an important part in the daily routine of the Moroccan people, and a good meal is regarded as the sign of a healthy life. The Moroccans are a proud and welcoming race, so chances are that you'll soon find yourself invited to dine with the family. If this is the case you should note that you'll probably find yourself eating with your hands, so don't use your left one as this is considered unclean and used for the toilet. Etiquette dictates that if you leave any food, it's a sign that you disliked the meal, while scraping you plate clean makes out that you didn't have enough! Finally, always be sure to praise the chef.

Typical dishes

Chicken is the most widely eaten meat in Morocco, with lamb or mutton second. Meat dishes are generally accompanied by fruit. Normally, there are five to six courses served at a traditional meal, and all produce is grown locally, meaning everything tastes fresh and flavoursome. Note that while vegetables are available every-where, a vegetarian will struggle with the local food as meat features in almost every dish.

Moroccan food generally revolves around salad, kebabs – typically skewered or minced lamb – and thick soups consisting of beans and pasta. For a more hearty meal, options include a stew (*tajine*) such as chicken, olive and lemon, or lamb, almonds and prunes, and also fish. Other typical dishes include couscous, which is served with meat, vegetables and fruit, or roasted lamb with paprika or cumin. On special occasions, the legendary Moroccan dish of *pastilla* is served. This is a pie of chicken or pigeon, which is served topped with pastry, almonds and icing sugar.

Moroccans eat three meals a day, and breakfast generally consists of a savoury pastry with meat or a semolina pancake, while lunch can be a *tajine* or couscous, with leftovers eaten for supper, sometimes with a salad or omelettes. Bread is eaten with every meal and is regarded as being sacred.

The street food served in Morocco is among the best in the world and there is a massive variety of choice. Among the delicacies on offer are minced lamb kebabs, lentils, chickpeas, olives, bread drizzled with honey, spicy snails and fritters with syrup. Vegetables, salads, preserved meats and bread are also sold, along with a *kefta* – seasoned minced lamb with salad and French fries, all served in bread.

Moroccans are also fond of sweet pastries and there are many cinnamon and almond-flavoured, crescent-shaped pastries dusted with icing sugar available. These were introduced by the French.

Drinks

Being an Islamic country, Muslims are forbidden to drink alcohol, although in practise it is still widely available in Morocco, both in restaurants and shops. During the French occupation, many vines where introduced into the country, and consequently there are some good rosés and light reds produced, especially around Fès and Meknès. Beer is also brewed in the country, the most well known being Flag Speciale or Stork.

However, the most popular Moroccan drink is mint tea. Sometimes known as 'Moroccan whiskey', it consists of Chinese tea, spearmint or *nanaa'* – sugar and boiling water. Mint tea has its own place in the meal structure, with three cups required to be drunk on the completion of your meal.

Almond milk is another one of Morocco's most famous beverages. Generally served after mint tea, it's made from a blend of almonds, rose water, orange-flower water, sugar and milk. You'll also find a variety of freshly squeezed fruit juices on sale from street vendors.

Recipe for Mint Tea
You'll need . . .
10 sprigs of fresh mint
3 teaspoons of green tea
3 tablespoons sugar
4 cups of water

How to make it . . .
1. Boil the water and pour a small amount into the teapot.
2. Add the mint, the green tea and sugar to the water, then fill with the remaining hot water.
3. Let the mix brew for three minutes.
4. Fill one glass with the tea, then pour it back into the pot. Do this a couple of times to allow the sugar to dissolve thoroughly.
5. Pour the tea into the glass from a height to achieve a foam.
6. Garnish with the remaining sprigs of mint.

THE CULTURE SHOCK

The culture in Morocco is undoubtedly going to take some getting used to. Being an Islamic country, the day's timetable is very much structured around the call to prayer, with the annual calendar peppered with religious celebrations such as Ramadan, which requires fasting for one month. However, while there are strict social customs in place that dictate everything from your behaviour to the lifestyle of women, foreigners will find that they are not tied by the same laws as the locals. That said it is important to recognise and be aware of the social customs that govern Moroccan life, especially if you are to be working and socialising with the Moroccan people.

21

While legally – thanks to the Mudawana, the family code law which was passed in 2004 – women enjoy equal rights with men, traditionally Moroccan women are not regarded as having the same freedoms or as being the equal of a man. However, behind closed doors the woman is the backbone of the family. At home she may remove her headscarf, which must be worn at all times when outside, and foreign women must be aware that in some circumstances they may be required to wear long sleeves and ankle-length trousers or skirts. However, Morocco is one of the most tolerant of Islamic countries when it comes to women, and in the larger cities this strictness is not always followed, especially as the King has implemented new laws in relation to women's rights.

Foreigners are regarded as – and generally are – wealthy compared to their Moroccan counterparts. Consequently, given that you are likely to earn as much in one month as a Moroccan will in a year, you will find that many of the locals will charge you more for goods and services than they would a Moroccan. However, this doesn't mean that the Moroccans aren't welcoming to foreigners – they simply see it as good business practice. Always think hard about what you are being asked to pay and don't just go along with it – you'll soon figure out what an average local/fair price is.

For the Moroccan people, family is the most important part of life, and so once behind closed doors in the bosom of the family, they dislike being disturbed, so never turn up unannounced. In order to help you settle into life in Morocco it is important to make friends with the locals and your neighbours, as this is the only way to feel accepted into the community. Moroccans will welcome you whole-heartedly into the community, and at first their interest may seem overwhelming – many foreigners have commented on the lack of privacy and personal space they are afforded – but this is normal, and if you can get used to it you will find that there is a real sense of community in every village, town and city. One interesting aspect of the Moroccan's welcoming nature towards strangers stems from their Islamic beliefs which state that Allah may appear among you at any time in the guise of a stranger. Consequently you will find yourself well looked after.

Finally, Islam creates a certain amount of fatalism among the locals, and so foreigners may find that the average Moroccan has what they would class as a very bleak view of life, believing that everything is decreed by Allah, so there is no point trying to change what is 'inevitable'. There is also a strong belief in djinns and the Evil Eye and you will probably see many signs designed to ward off evil.

Moving to or buying a property in Morocco, needs to be something that is done by the adventurous investor, and someone who is willing to give life in an Islamic country a fair go – remember, you're not buying in southern Spain or the Dordogne where there's the comfort blanket of having an English family around every corner. In Morocco you need to be prepared to immerse yourself in a culture and community that is totally different and in many cases alien to you. Should you embrace it, you'll find yourself well rewarded.

Dance and folklore

Morocco has a diverse and fascinating folklore, which is as varied as the people and landscape of the country. Much of this is expressed in dance and music as well as the exotic and colourful costumes worn. At the Marrakesh Folklore Festival the following dances occur which hark back to ancient times and incorporate symbology deemed undecipherable today:

◆ **The Awash**   Originating from the High Atlas and Ouarzazate areas, the dance begins with women in colourful dresses and a group of men sitting around a fire. The silence is broken by a high-pitched cry as the men begin to beat their drums and the women sway slowly from side to side. Gradually their movements increase with the rhythm until they reach a frenzied finale.

◆ **The Ouais**   Set to ancient music, this ballet-like dance includes an orchestra comprising a single-stringed fiddle and a number of three-stringed, turtle-shell mandolins. These accompany the dancers, who wear brightly coloured kaftans. It's a simple dance with only a few steps, but as the couples alternate their steps it becomes increasingly intricate.

◆ **The Ait Atta**   Similar to the Awash dance, this dance marks the end of the working season. A row of women face a row of men, and dance using gestures which show their joy at the end of the working season.

◆ **The Ait Bodar** This dance encompasses the belief that ancient warriors had to act as one in order to secure victory. A row of men wearing white *gandoras* link arms and chant their song while moving together as one unit.

◆ **Ha Ha** A flute is the only instrument used in this dance, which comprises a group of men who stamp their feet and clap their hands in unison. This dance requires incredible precision.

◆ **The Fantasia** Performed entirely on horseback, a procession of women marks the start of the event, followed by men who enter wearing their tribal emblem and riding in order of rank. Once the procession is complete the The Aid el Broud (Festival of Gunpowder) begins with intense gunfire. Horsemen then ride in their ranks shouting and shooting until the grand finale which is marked by the shooting of their *moukhahla* rifles.

MOROCCO'S TOURIST DEVELOPMENT

The development of tourism is the key aim of the ambitious Plan Azur, designed to transform the country into an economic power-house. The plan aims to increase tourism to ten million visitors by 2010, which will in turn generate 20% of the country's GDP. In order to achieve this the government has planned major investment in transport, facilities and services, including the introduction of new tourism opportunities such as golf. This has required an investment of $10 billion from the government, which aims to provide 160,000 new beds, thus bringing the national capacity in the country to 230,000 tourist beds. It also aims to create some 600,000 new jobs. Naturally, the property market will be a direct beneficiary of these positive developments in tourism and as visitor numbers and interest in the country grows, so will investment in bricks and mortar.

Moroccan tourism has been growing steadily since the turn of the century, largely thanks to the implementation of Plan Azur. Visitor numbers stood at 6.5 million in 2006, a rise of 12% on the previous year, with tourist numbers up by 18% in 2007, with 4.3 million people visiting the country in the first seven months of the year. Consequently, revenue generated from tourism rose by 30% to reach 53 billion dirhams (approximately £3.2 billion) in 2006.

The revitalising of the tourist trade has been made possible thanks to the adoption of an Open Skies policy which has attracted a large number of low-cost airlines to the country's airports. There are also plans in place to build 50 new hotels, new marinas, golf courses and a number of luxury residential properties, most of which will be focused around the six new developments currently under construction (see Chapter 2 on Where To Buy for more details). This is set to further bolster tourist expansion in the run up to 2010.

During the summer of 2006, flight bookings to Marrakesh rose by an incredible 295% compared to the previous year. According to ONDA – the Moroccan Airport Authority – Moroccan airports served some 32,935 flights during the first quarter of 2007, compared to 29,482 in the same period of 2006. Today, there are already 100 flights a week in operation between the UK and Marrakesh, and with Morocco only being eight miles from southern Spain, it's easy to fly into Cadiz or Málaga and travel across to Morocco. This, plus the promised construction of an underwater tunnel linking Morocco and Spain, has resulted in a rise in interest and investment in the Moroccan property market, and knowing exactly where cheap flights are currently travelling to, and where new routes will open up, is key to investment success.

GETTING THERE, FLIGHTS AND AIRPORTS

By air

The best way to reach Morocco is to fly, unless you have time to spare, in which case driving down through France and Spain can be an enjoyable experience. There are now regular low-cost flights into Morocco, with easyJet offering services from London Gatwick to Marrakesh and from Madrid and Lyon to Casablanca. Ryanair also offers flights from London Luton to Marrakesh and Fès. British Airways flies directly from Heathrow and Gatwick into Marrakesh and Casablanca, with seasonal flights to Agadir and Tangier.

Low-cost airline Atlas Blue also offers flights from London Gatwick into Marrakesh, while Royal Air Maroc offers flights from London to numerous destinations throughout Morocco. These services have also all become cheaper in the last couple of years, and while charter flights can offer good value for money, the budget airlines are today more competitive than they used to be.

Other options include flying into airports such as Cadiz or Málaga in Spain, and then travelling by ferry into Morocco. See the section on arriving by car/ferry below for more details.

Morocco's three main international airports are Casablanca, Tangier and Agadir, although there are growing numbers of flights into Marrakesh as airport expansion gets underway (visit www.onda.ma for a guide to Morocco's airports). Plan Azur has promised an improvement to airport services, with new airports to be built or upgrades offered on existing facilities. Most importantly, Oujda Airport on the Mediterranean Coast, close to Saïdia, is now being upgraded due to Morocco's recently announced Open Skies initiative, which aims to bring low-cost European airlines to the airport at some point in 2008. The Open Skies policy has encouraged many new routes to be opened from throughout Europe and easyJet now flies daily to Marrakesh, with further routes to be announced shortly, including an expected service to Tangier. Meanwhile, Ryanair has signed a deal to open up 20 new routes over the next five years.

Useful websites

www.easyjet.co.uk
www.ryanair.com
www.atlas-blue.com
www.britishairways.com
www.royalairmaroc.com
www.onda.ma

By car/ferry

If you're willing to drive into France or even get down to the south of Spain, you'll find that there are numerous ferry options to transport you on to Morocco. The journey can be an enjoyable experience and a chance to tour many sites in France and Spain should you wish. It can be done in two days if necessary, or two weeks should you so please. The best route is to take the ferry or Eurostar into France. From Calais, it's 2242.9 km (24 hours' solid drive) down to Tarifa in Spain. For a more personalised route, visit www.theaa.com and select their route planner.

From Sète in the south of France, you can secure a 36-hour crossing to Tangier all year round. From Spain, there are high-speed ferries available from Tarifa (they take 35 minutes), Algeciras and Gibraltar, while there are also crossings from Almeria and Málaga to Melilla (Spanish Morocco), which take about six to nine hours. There are also high-speed options to travel to Ceuta (Spanish Morocco) from Algeciras. Visit www.southernferries.co.uk/moroccoferries.htm to find out more about routes, prices and bookings. It's advisable to book a place during the peak season.

The Morocco tunnel

Part of Plan Azur includes plans to build a tunnel between Spain and Morocco, linking the two countries and making access even easier. The idea of this has been circulating since the 1970s, although no actual progress was made until recent years. At the start of 2008, the Spanish Development Ministry stated on the record that two adjacent tunnels will be built to run beneath the Straits of Gibraltar to Morocco. The plan is for them to run from Punta Paloma, 40 km west of Gibraltar, to Punta Malabata near Tangiers. If construction goes ahead, it will have an enormous impact on property values, tourism and trade, especially in the immediate area surrounding Tangier. The tunnel will stretch for 39 km – with 27.7 km being under the sea – and construction is set to start in 2008, although it will be 20 years before work is finally completed, at a cost of €5,000 million.

2
What to buy in Morocco

Morocco offers a real range of properties for the potential buyer, from newly built apartments to run-down riads for renovation. Most demand is for property in the coastal resort developments or in the medinas, although interest is growing for modern apartments in urban centres such as Tangiers and Casablanca.

Traditional homes complete with patterned tiles, intricate ironwork, carved arches and delicate minarets can be found in Morocco, although in many cases, family homes may not possess these, and while we Europeans yearn for spacious rooms and windows, the Moroccans prefer foot-thick doors, walled gardens and tiny windows, opting to keep their family life quite literally behind closed doors. It is also worth noting that the Moroccans themselves – as with many Eastern Europeans – would prefer a newly built apartment to a ruined riad, and are quite happy to get shot of these crumbling old buildings, putting them on the market and then moving into the new town areas of cities such as Fès and Marrakesh.

It is important also to realise that there is a massive divide between the old and the new in Morocco, and the facilities available in each. Housing ranges from the traditional to the ultramodern and luxurious, although in rural areas you'll find that many Moroccans still live in ksour and agricultural villages, with a poor standard of living. Despite efforts by the government to renovate and modernise the traditional medinas, access to public utilities in some centres still remains limited. For example, within the walls of a medina you'll find that you will be unlikely to have a proper bathroom, with only a tap and basic toilet (not a sit-down, or Western toilet). There will also be few plugs and sockets for electricals, probably no telephone line and a very basic kitchen. In contrast, buying in the Ville Nouveau will give you these things, as well as a modern property – but at a price. With a more Western home comes Western-style prices. All these things need to be taken into consideration when it comes to choosing where and what to buy.

Below is a round up of the different property types you can purchase and the pros and cons of buying them.

OLD PROPERTIES AND RENOVATIONS

Medinas

The fad for buying a typically Moroccan medina property to renovate has piqued the interest of many a British DIY enthusiast, as it once did – and still does – in Italy with the stone-built *casa colonica* (farmhouses). What is so special about the medinas in Morocco – they are found in many North African countries – is that they preserve a traditionally medieval way of life, and this appeals to many foreign buyers. Medinas are essentially the walled quarters of a town or city that would have been fortified against attack. All have immense gates, known as babs, and are split into quartiers (neighbourhoods), each of which provides amenities such as public baths, a mosque and a school for local residents. Typically, the choice of homes here varies hugely, ranging from one-room mud-walled shacks to palatial villas and houses. However, uniformity can be seen in the colour, with most northern medians being whitewashed, while the southern ones are the same reddish-brown as the soil in the region.

Medinas are traffic free – save for donkeys – but with narrow, maze-like streets, they're also 'map-free' – be prepared to wander the streets aimlessly before you get your bearings. You're likely to pass numerous mosques, palaces and souks before ending up back where you started!

Living in a medina will land you slap bang in the middle of local Moroccan life, so be prepared for bustle and noise as this is what gives the medina its character and makes it such a sought after location – after all, this is an area where Moroccans work, live and pray.

There are downsides to buying in a medina. For a start they're old, which won't come as a shock, but this means that walls may be crumbling, sewage variable and rubbish and pollution a problem. They may also appear claustrophobic to many, so if you prefer wide open spaces and peace and quiet, then buying within a medina is not for you. Other problems stem from the fact that 99% of all properties within a medina are not titled. However, you can purchase a new title, although this will set you back an additional 2.5% of the value of the property, and – more importantly – a lot of time and red tape.

Despite these negatives, there are many advantages to buying within a medina, most notably the unique properties you will find, the many cultural attractions and the possibility of securing a healthy rental income. Other positives include the sense of community you will feel from living within a medina, and the option it gives you to appreciate and become part of a different lifestyle. Medinas are also in demand and property generally scarce, so they offer good appreciation rates. However, in most cases you will find that you will have to restore or modernise the property in some way, unless you buy a pre-renovated resale.

Riads

Thanks to a new vogue for renovating property in Marrakesh, buying a riad has become a fashionable pastime. A riad is a traditional Moroccan house or palace, which has its own interior garden, around which are built the rooms of the house, often with a balcony overlooking the garden. Many have now been renovated and act as hotels, restaurants or short-term rental accommodation. Canny investors have also bought riads while prices were low, done them up and then sold them on to foreign buyers now that supply has become limited and demand high. Consequently, there are habitable and renovated riads out there ready to buy, although they are selling fast.

Unlike modern properties, riads follow no set interior layout and all are different or quirky in some way – from the size and shape, to layout of the rooms and position of doors and windows. In many instances this is why they are popular, as each riad is unique, although the rooms tend to be narrow and the ceilings high. However, in many cases the exterior colour is always the same – for example, whitewashed walls with blue shutters in Essaouira or the distinctive red of Marrakesh's medina.

While there are many positives to buying a characterful riad – the cheap price, the location, the opportunity to own a unique property – there are things you need to be aware of. The first is the possibility that you will end up owning a property that will cost the same amount to renovate – or in some cases more – than it did to buy in the first place. So, if you do intend to buy a run-down riad, you need to be prepared to fork out the cash to modernise it – especially in places such as Marrakesh, Essaouira and, increasingly, Fès, as demand for builders and artisans is extremely high. You also need to be aware of any zoning or building regulations.

Secondly, most riad properties don't have titles, meaning that you will need to secure one, plus you'll have to be prepared to invest the time in tracking down the current family owners and securing the approval of all of them, before the sale can go ahead. This can often be a stumbling block for many people. The easiest way to buy a riad is often to invest in a second generation, fully renovated one, complete with title, although this is not to everyone's taste, as many people like to put their own stamp on their property.

In many cases, new developments are now building replica riads to meet the demand for character properties from foreign buyers; for example, you can buy a fully furnished riad with two bedrooms in Marrakesh for £101,000 (1,447,996 dirhams).

Insider info

Frances McKay, of estate agent Francophiles, explains why her clients find riads so appealing.

A riad is an old, traditional Moroccan house located within the ramparts of the medina, and the most popular cities to buy a riad in are Marrakesh, Fès and Essaouira. Typically, the entrance to the riad is through a solid, wooden front door. On the other side of the door lies an oasis of peace and calm, deliberately a far cry from the hurly-burly of the medina. A large, rectangular patio planted with bougainvillea and jasmine – and often with a central fountain – is surrounded by high-ceilinged rooms. Most riads have two floors with a balcony on the upper floor which looks down over the patio. On top of the first floor there might also be a rooftop terrace, and in Marrakesh these can offer stunning views of the Koutoubia mosque and the snow-covered Atlas Mountains – a marvellous bonus. The architectural style of riads in Fès is opulent, with mosaic walls and floor tiles (*zelliges*), stucco plasterwork, stained glass windows and wrought-iron balconies. In Marrakesh the interiors are simpler – walls are finished in *Tadelakt*, a polished plaster, and carved, intricate cedar wood doors and woodwork abound. Essaouira is renowned for its blue shutters and whitewashed walls. Inside, white walls are traditional, *thuya* wood is used for carvings, and ironwork for balconies. Regardless of the city, furnishings are very exotic and comfortable.

Dar

In some cases, you may hear a riad being referred to as a dar. This simply means it is a less grand version of a riad, being smaller and lacking a garden.

Kasbah

Within a medina you can also find the kasbah, a unique fortified area or fortress, where the ruler or leader of the community would live. The walls are high, and the kasbah positioned on a hill, in a strategic position to keep it safe from attack. Many of the popular areas to buy within a medina are situated around the kasbah area.

One of the finest preserved examples in Morocco is in Aït Benhaddou. While most people settle for buying in or around a kasbah, some people are willing to buy a whole fortress – most notably Richard Branson, who transformed his into a luxury hotel. In most cases you'll find that a Kasbah is too big – and too expensive – for a single family, but if you are looking to start a tourist business in Morocco, a kasbah might be just the thing. However, be aware that you'll come across the same title problems here as you would with a riad, not to mention the renovation costs!

NEW PROPERTIES AND DEVELOPMENTS

Ville Nouvelle

Many of Morocco's larger towns and cities, as well as having a medina, also have a new town area, often introduced during the French protectorate. These new towns generally offer newly built apartment properties and are modern in their layout, often employing wide, French-style boulevards and art deco buildings dating back to the 1930s. Most buyers here tend to be foreigners, and in many cases retirees who are seeking a western-style home rather than something traditionally Moroccan. However, many Moroccans are also keen to upgrade from what they see as a run-down riad, to something more comfortable and modern, so when they can, many are moving into these new areas.

Each Ville Nouvelle offers an abundance of amenities and facilities, including shops, restaurants, bars and schools, while on the outskirts you'll find larger villas. The appeal of buying in a Ville Nouvelle is generally that property is modern, fully habitable, in some cases fitted and furnished, and ready to move into. The titles are clean and the homes offer more space and only require one payment – no worrying about renovation costs. However, you may not have that much more peace and quiet, as cars are allowed in these areas and the roads can be jam-packed. What's more, there is generally a lot of development happening around the Ville Nouvelles.

Apartments

There has been a massive boom in the development of apartments in recent years, largely down to the growth of foreign demand, but also because the Moroccans themselves would rather live in a brand spanking new property than an old riad. Many new developments are springing up throughout the country as Plan Azur gets into full swing and today a number of wealthy Moroccans and Spaniards own holiday apartments along the southern Atlantic or Mediterranean coasts, using them as a weekend retreat. Consequently, this high demand means that those owning land in a sought-after construction belt can sell at a premium.

The Moroccans have always limited the number of storeys in apartment buildings, and generally you'll find they are only three floors high. Some are growing to between five and seven, but no more than that.

Apartment styles vary depending on where you are looking to purchase. Most foreigners are keen to buy within a development where there are onsite amenities, such as a pool, spa, gym and maintenance. However, most apartment blocks have a similar community upkeep system to Spain, meaning that if you own a home here, you have to pay an annual/monthly fee to help cover the costs of gardening, cleaning, caretaking, etc. Most apartment blocks will elect a manager, and in large developments, the developer themselves will oversee the upkeep and take the fee in return for their services. In an urban apartment block, the residents usually elect a manager from among their group who will be paid a monthly fee from the other residents to oversee the maintenance of the building.

In city areas, you may find that apartments are plain and functional – in other areas, they may be lavish and expansive. Deciding what

and where to buy is simply a case of thoroughly checking developments and properties and deciding what you want as the buyer.

There are many advantages to buying an apartment. For a start you
can lock it up and leave it. It will come with a title and will be fully
habitable – if it doesn't, don't buy as the chances are the developer
never obtained the title or permission to build, and so the property
won't actually belong to you. Other positives mean you won't have
to fork our for renovation costs and you will only have one outlay
of cash to arrange. Many apartments also come fully furnished and
with onsite amenities and extras; the rentals market will also be
strong. Finally, demand is high and as the resales market is so
strong, you are more than likely to make a good appreciation on
your investment.

The downsides are that most apartments are in modern surroundings rather than traditional Moroccan neighbourhoods and they
aren't characterful or unique properties, although there are cases of
some larger riads being split into apartments. Buying an apartment
also means you run the risk of buying into an expat or foreign
enclave rather than being able to enjoy life among the local
community.

Insider info

Frances McKay of Francophiles takes a look at the style of apartments on offer
throughout Morocco.

Newly built apartments are plentiful in the large towns and cities of Morocco.
There are several apartment blocks in the Guéliz and Hivernage districts of
Marrakesh, with more planned for the future. These are very European in design
and generally offer light and airy rooms, complete with bay windows which lead
onto a balcony or terrace. Most have air conditioning and well-equipped kitchens,
often with marble flooring and tiled bathrooms. A two-bedroom apartment with
two en-suite bathrooms is pretty much the norm, together with a fireplace,
balcony, garage, videophone and digicode. The more luxurious apartment blocks
can offer swimming pools on the roof of the building, in order to take advantage of
the views of the Atlas Mountains. Communal gardens are often included, and
these are always well tended and offer privacy.

There are also large developments under construction along the coastal fringes of the Mediterranean and the Atlantic. These developments offer modern, comfortable apartments in a complex complete with facilities such as swimming pools, 18-hole golf courses, supermarket, bars, restaurants, watersports and a marina – all with sea views. Access to the developments on the north Atlantic coast and in the Ceuta and Tetouan region is generally via Tangier with its fast ferry service to Spain and international airport, which is under construction. The more easterly development of Saïdia on the Mediterranean coast is accessed from Spain via the airport at Melilla, although with Oujda airport in the process of being expanded, you will soon be able to fly directly into the region.

Villas

In the suburbs, on the coast and on the outskirts of conurbations, you'll find there is plenty of room for villas, and they are generally surrounded by palm trees and located on quiet roads where traffic, shops and bars are scarce or non-existent. In many cases, people are buying land and constructing their own villas, although increasingly developers are seeing the potential with the foreign market to develop newly built villas within the newer developments. Affluent Moroccans are also keen on villas, especially as they are seen as a sign of wealth in the country.

There are two types of villa found in Morocco: the European-style villa and the Moroccan villa. As mentioned earlier, the Moroccans like their privacy and so a traditional Moroccan villa will be surrounded by gates or a wall, and is likely to be inaccessible from the road. Obviously, Moroccan villas are currently the more common type, although as developers are securing a foothold in the country, the demand for the Western-style villa is growing.

Your average Moroccan villa will have a small garden, a pool – again, this will be small – a terrace, balcony and a garage. It will also be arranged over three storeys (including the basement). The roof will be flat, the location quiet and the price will be affordable in relation to the UK and Spanish markets. In contrast, your European-style villa will offer more space for a garden and pool and blend traditional Moroccan features with modern design and fittings. There has been a growth in the number of gated communities springing up, and these have the added benefit of being 'lock up and leave', perfect for a holiday as well as rentals.

One thing that nearly all Moroccan properties suffer from is a lack of views – Moroccans simply don't put any stock in the concept of a 'room with a view', so unless you buy through a developer or build your own home, you are unlikely to find yourself overlooking a stunning coastline. Many Europeans have built their own personalised villas over the years, and the coastline around Essaouira is evidence of this, as well as being the result of many Europeans seeking more space and peace after living for a few years among the bustle and noise of the medinas.

Buying off-plan in developments

As part of Plan Azur, six new developments have sprung up along Morocco's coastline, creating a new and growing demand for off-plan property and the many new residential homes being constructed. Consequently, there have been increasing numbers of agents selling off-plan apartments and villas to foreign buyers, most of which sit within complexes complete with leisure and sports facilities, shops, bars, restaurants and luxury hotels. Morocco is a hotbed for developments, thanks to government incentives and the wealth of land available for purchase at reasonable prices. Many developments are springing up within the suburban areas, or on the main routes out of the country's largest cities, such as Marrakesh and Fès. As already mentioned, there are also the developments being built on the Atlantic and Mediterranean coast, meaning there is no lack of choice for investors. Off-plan properties have also appreciated well, with prices nearly doubling in recent years as demand has skyrocketed – and so you can be sure you're making a sound investment, especially as many of these developments offer guaranteed rentals.

The last couple of years have seen this market grow as safeguards are put in place to protect a buyer's investment. Developers now have to prove that they have 50% of the money required to construct the planned properties prior to commencing the build. The buyer also needs to be presented with a VEFA contract signed by the developer. This was introduced in 2002 in order to protect the buyer from the 'black market' developer, and is highly protective of the investor. For more details on buying an off-plan property, see Chapter 6, on the buying process.

Insider Info

Steve Burns, Marketing Manager of Compass Properties, offers some top tips on buying in a development.

If you are going to buy in a purpose-built development, it is wise to take advantage of the numerous subsidised trips offered by Compass and others. These will provide you not only with the opportunity to see the properties, but also to see the country, view the development location and experience the culture and facilities first-hand.

The critical point to confirm is that the developer (a) owns the land or property to be sold – i.e. has the title, and (b) that all necessary permits have been obtained for construction. It is essential to use an English-speaking lawyer (or notary), as many documents will be written in Arabic. Reputable developers will be able to provide the names of appropriately qualified firms.

Most new developments are sold off-plan and are subject to stage payments. Initial deposits tend to be around 40%, with the balance payable on completion. Mortgages are available for up to 70% of the purchase price in Morocco, but it may be cheaper to raise the money in the UK.

Property investment guaranteed

There are all sorts of incentives in place to encourage you to buy in Morocco, not least of all the guaranteed rental income scheme complete with tax incentives. Some companies even offer money-back guarantees, such as the developers of the Moroccan-style resort the Gardens of Fedala. It promises a 100% buy back guarantee should you decide to sell your property within nine years, as well as a 7% net rental guarantee for the same period – which equates to an income of some €13,000 a year. You are also guaranteed to receive the price you paid for your property in full should you decide to sell, thus undercutting any risk you may be worried you are taking by investing in Morocco. However, any potential investors in a scheme such as this should ensure they see proof that they will be guaranteed such levels of rental income, and must check that all terms are included in any contract, to avoid losing out.

Leaseback

Buying a property leaseback is a system that is becoming increasing popular and is now being employed in most countries in the world. In operation for over 20 years, it originated in France, quickly spread to Spain and is now being introduced in Morocco. This is regarded as a safe and easy way to own a home overseas and the concept is simple.

1. An investor buys the freehold of a property outright and then leases it back to a management company for renewable periods of up to ten years.
2. The property owner will receive a guaranteed rental return for the property every year, irrespective of occupancy, at a fixed amount, which in many cases can offset – or at least contribute towards – the cost of their mortgage payments. Community fees and maintenance costs are normally paid by the property management company.
3. At the end of the leaseback period, the owner of the property can either decide to live in the property, sell the property or simply sign a new leaseback contract with the management company for another fixed period of guaranteed income.

The advantages of the leaseback scheme are that you end up owning a property overseas – essentially a nest egg for the future – which is making you money and helping to cover your costs. You can expect to generate between 2.5% and 6% per annum from renting your home through the agency, and it also means that you don't have to worry about maintaining or renting the property out. At the end of the lease you are left with a property that can be yours or continue to be used to generate income – at no point do you have to worry

New build vs old property

New build		Old property	
Pros	**Cons**	**Pros**	**Cons**
◆ Have a fully habitable, ready-to-move into home ◆ You may well get furnishings and fittings included in the final price ◆ Your newly built or modern property will come with a title ◆ In many cases amenities will be on site in the case of a development, or nearby ◆ If within a development you will find you can attract many holiday lets or even be offered guaranteed rental income ◆ Once you have paid the full amount your property is worth, you won't have to worry about renovation costs	◆ You have to wait an average of one year to occupy if you buy off-plan ◆ A newly built property often lacks character and has no traditional Moroccan elements ◆ You will generally find that you are buying in an area with many foreigners, rather than a local community	◆ You can design and rebuild/renovate a personalised and traditional property, which is unique ◆ You will generally find that you are going to be living within a Moroccan community ◆ A unique riad property will secure you more rental, especially if in a traditionally Moroccan area or Medina	◆ You have to be prepared to spend more on renovation, as most Moroccan properties will need modernisation ◆ Most old traditional properties won't have a title, so it will take time and money to secure one and OK the sale ◆ Builders and artisans can be in short supply and can be expensive ◆ You won't be able to move in immediately in many cases as most old properties are not fully habitable

about the property falling into disrepair. As your home is being 'used' during the rental period, it is a good way to cover costs and make money.

Obviously, the disadvantage is that you don't have the option to use it for holidays during the period of the lease, except within a six-week window, which could well be during the low peak, bad weather months. However, given that you will pay no VAT and benefit from no capital gains payments at the end of the lease should you wish to sell, this is a great scheme to secure good returns on your investment. You can buy a one-bedroom property on the Route d'Amizmiz highway out of Marrakesh, with an 11-year lease offering a 5.5% return per annum for £114,618 (1,643,198 dirhams).

LAND AND RURAL PROPERTIES

Land

The sale of land is currently big business in Morocco, especially as there are so many developments underway with prices so low on the outskirts of cities such as Fès and Marrakesh, attracting many foreign buyers keen on building their own home. However, purchasing land is not a straightforward procedure for foreigners in Morocco.

Land has been designated into different zones:

◆ Residential/Constructible

◆ Agricultural

◆ Religious

◆ Military

◆ Industrial

◆ Touristique

◆ Government

◆ Unzoned

Land laws in Morocco are still very patchy, and from region to region, classification and usage varies, as does whether you can buy land, let alone build on it. If you intend to buy land in Morocco, be prepared for a bit of a rollercoaster ride!

The general rule states that foreigners cannot buy land outside the urban perimeter of a town or city. However, in order to attract investors, the Moroccan State has introduced a law by which you can legally change the classification of land from Agricultural to Residential (Constructible), thus allowing foreigners to purchase it. Investors need to apply for a VNA (Vocation Non Agricole – see Chapter 6 for more details). The procedure is quite complex and needs to have authorisation from a number of different authorities – the local town hall, the urban agency, the Wilaya (regional government office), the CRI, etc. – and an architect and a surveyor will have to be appointed. While this is certainly a speedier process than pre 2005, foreigners still need to be prepared for a long wait. Buyers are also required to buy no less than one hectare of land to apply for a VNA (this again varies from region to region).

One final complication is the title, which may well be non-existent, as with many traditional riads. Any paperwork that does exist will refer to the land perimeters as stretching from one landmark to another, rather than actually detailing the size of the parcel of land as a measurement; it will also always be in Arabic. Consequently – as with an untitled property – you will need to track down all family members in order to get the go-ahead to purchase. That said, if you can see the process through then you will find you can purchase in remote areas that offer some stunning views and surrounding countryside – and you can buy as much land as you like.

If you buy within the urban perimeter then land will be titled and no permit will have to be applied for, as most land will be zoned as Constructible or Touristique, allowing you to build on it. While there are advantages of buying within an urban area, land is selling fast and there will be restrictions on what you can build, the size you can build to and also the style of the property; it will also be more costly. That said, it will be quicker, easier and simpler to connect to utilities within an urban area and to start building. The general rule of thumb is that you can buy one hectare for a residential home, and for anything larger you will have to prove that it is for a tourist-related venture – for example, a hotel – in order for the purchase to go ahead.

The registration fees (stamp duty) for purchasing land are between 2.5% and 5%, while the notary fees are around 1%. The purchase price is inclusive of VAT.

Rural properties

In most cases you will find that if you are looking to buy a rural or farmhouse property, you will be buying agricultural land, so will have to apply for a VNA (see Chapter 6 on buying land). There will also be the added renovation costs and, more than likely, you won't be connected to utilities. All these issues will have to be sensibly weighed up in terms of cost, time and effort, and how much of each you are prepared to give the project.

Rural properties are generally very basic square buildings, similar to riads in terms of their layout but with very few amenities, such as a toilet. Water and electricity can be difficult to get hold of, so you may well have to look at options like solar power, and if you are looking at the more remote mountainous regions, while you may have a well, you'll have to consider the limitations a lack of electricity will cause – during the winter months your solar panels will be of little use. The government is working hard to introduce water, sewage and electricity across the country, but currently only two-thirds of the population are guaranteed these facilities.

Before buying, you need to take into account the infrastructure, the remote location, lack of amenities and facilities – such as shops, schools and hospitals – and the extremes of climate. There are also the language considerations to be aware of in the more remote communities.

While there are attractions to living in the countryside, with stunning, unspoilt views, you need to be aware that not only will you have to renovate, but you'll also have to negotiate the red-tape and secure permits to transform the land into Residential/Contructible land in order to buy. Clearly, buying in rural Morocco is certainly harder compared to buying on the perimeters of a town or city, but if you have the patience to see it through, you can end up owning and living in a truly unique and stunning location, and within the heart of a genuine Moroccan community.

However, be aware that within the local community, you will be regarded as the wealthy foreigner, which is what you will be in relation to the levels of poverty some Moroccans live in. While you will more than likely be welcomed into the community, you may well find you are constantly asked for favours. Be prepared for this – it's not the lifestyle for everyone and the demands may soon become unwelcome.

Coastal properties

There has been a growing demand for coastal properties, and in many cases these are the most popular option for foreign buyers. Thanks to Plan Azur, parts of the 3,500 km of coastline are being carefully developed, offering a wealth of newly built apartments, villas and duplexes to choose from.

Other than newly built developments, there are some more traditional housing options such as small riads, although these might be slightly inland as opposed to directly on the coast – the Moroccans generally aren't big on sea views. There is also the option to buy land and build, although in every case the zoning and regulations surrounding the purchase are likely to be different – see the above section on land for more details.

45

The main concern when buying on the coast will be the chance that developers may build close to, or in front of your property, so always check if there are any building plans in place with the Land Registry (Conservation Foncière). It is also important to be aware of the fact that the coastline is damp and salt erosion can be a problem – as can the high winds that batter the Atlantic Coast and make it such a surfing hotspot.

Before buying, it's also important to check if a beach is public or private, belonging to a nearby hotel or development, as this will stop you from using it and consequently eradicate many of the benefits of buying there. Finally, there are the problems with pollution and rubbish, with some beaches being littered and dirty; on the other hand, many are remote and pristine, so always make sure you do your homework and research the area thoroughly before committing to buy.

Despite all the negatives, living on the coast is the ideal location for many foreign buyers, with stunning views, expansive beaches to swim and sunbathe on, and the chance to secure some healthy rental income. One of the biggest reasons to buy along the coast is the promotion the Moroccan government is giving the coastal regions in an effort to boost tourism, and consequently the demand for rentals.

Currently, property and land are still affordable and there is a wealth of choice. Check out your potential location – do you want bars and restaurants? If so, you'll have to look at the more developed resorts rather than one of the many small towns and fishing villages dotted along the coast. If you are buying purely as an investment, look to one of the up-and-coming Plan Azur resorts, which will have all the facilities and amenities on hand and be a prime holiday destination. Whether you are buying a holiday home, a property to live in or to rent, there are many plus points to owning a home on the seafront.

3
Where to buy in Morocco

Morocco is famed for its desert interiors, to the point where many envision it as a sandy, arid country. However, this simply isn't the case, and thanks to the many government initiatives and development schemes, people are beginning to realise that there is much more to Morocco than that – many areas are lush and green, with vast tracts of sandy beaches and mountain interiors. Here is an overview of Morocco's 16 regions, to help you get to grips with the country.

AN OVERVIEW OF THE PROPERTY MARKET

Thanks to the Moroccan government's effort to revitalise and diversify the economy, by investing in the infrastructure, encouraging tourism and their determination to combat inflation and promote overseas investment, Morocco has been transformed into one of the most successful emerging markets in the world.

Why Morocco?

Morocco is currently on the cusp of a property boom, experiencing price appreciation rates of between 10% and 50% over the last 12 months, and 280% since 2001. Property currently retails at one-third of Spanish levels, with prices ranging from £70,000 for an apartment to £150,000 for a riad to renovate. Morocco has become a viable investment option to residents of western and eastern European markets. As a short haul yet comparatively exotic destination,

Morocco offers year-round sunshine and has a forward-thinking government and King, who are keen to transform the country into a modern and westernised destination. £2.2 billion is being invested to transform the country into a leading tourist centre, with six new coastal resorts being created through Vision 2010 – also known as Plan Azur. Culturally different, this isn't your average bucket and spade or fish and chips destination, and while it won't appeal to everyone this is a major draw for many, especially as the desire for an authentic, traditional investment location grows among buyers tired of the expat enclaves of the Costa del Sols of this world. The affordability of the country, with prices a fraction of those of Spain and France, adds to the already strong appeal of the country, especially as the next two to three years are expected to see continued appreciation rates of 15% to 20%. The Open Skies policy guarantees the continuation of budget flights, which if anything are only set to grow thanks to the airport development and expansion scheme in place. Morocco offers skiing in the Atlas Mountains, an expansive coastline complete with white sandy beaches, plus ancient cities, great food and a fascinating culture. With such an intoxicating blend of reasons to buy here, it's unsurprising that Morocco is tipped to be such a massive investment market.

Property prices

Over the last few years Morocco has seen growth of anything between 15% to 50% per annum. Average property prices in the country vary hugely given the diversity of locations, but the average newly built one-bedroom apartment starts from £100,000 (1,520,421 dirhams). However, in the centre of Marrakesh you could spend anything up to £745,527 (11,338,990 dirhams) for a renovated riad as demand is astronomical.

Still, prices are around half the price of other European hotspots such as Spain, France and Italy, and a one-bedroom apartment in Morocco can cost as little as £596 (9,061 dirhams) per square metre, compared to £1,491 (22,664 dirhams) in southern Spain. What's more, the cost of living is comparatively low. As a result, the market has grown by around 50% to 75% since 2001, with new developers moving in from Dubai and Europe, offering excellent investment opportunities.

Average property prices

One-bedroom apartment: £66,912 (1,017,116 dirhams)
Two-bedroom apartment: £78,900 (1,199,285 dirhams)
Three-bedroom villa: £208,067 (3,162,633 dirhams)

Who's buying here?

If you choose to invest in the potential of the Moroccan property market, you will certainly be in good company. According to the *Financial Times*, 'Morocco is experiencing a booming property market, and one particular area of growth is luxury property.' Richard Branson, Malcolm Forbes, David Beckham and members of The Rolling Stones are just some of the world's rich and famous who have bought property in the country, keeping its media profile high and helping to fuel awareness and demand within the market.

Primarily, buyers tend to be purchasing purely for investment, thanks to the high rates of appreciation, and while the big bucks have already been made over the last five to ten years, you can still expect to generate healthy returns as long as you are prepared to buy long term. This isn't the place to buy off-plan and sell before completion, making a killing the process. Today, Morocco is more the place to buy and hold on to your property for a good few years. As more and more luxury self-contained resorts, such as Mediterrania Saïdia, continue to be constructed, you will find more holiday-home buyers here.

Rental opportunities

As Morocco is a country which is currently trying to build its economy on the basis of tourism, and given the levels of development being undertaken in order to encourage tourist growth, you can be sure to reap the rewards for investing here. Rental occupancy rates are high, reaching 85% most years. Consequently, you can expect to secure healthy rental returns of around 10%, with no shortage of demand for character properties or coastal homes.

The future

As the market looks set to continue developing at a healthy rate for the next few years, Morocco represents an excellent investment, and one where you can see your property appreciate in value by up to 50% in some areas, and where rental returns will be high. While it is always difficult to predict what will happen in the future, given the high levels of investment and government dedication to securing foreign investment and expanding tourism, there doesn't seem to be any reason to worry about a drop in fortunes. It is believed that the market will continue to grow at a similar rate as presently experienced until the completion of the 2010 project and the six new developments. At this point, the market may see a settling of prices.

Insider info

Adam Cornwell, Managing Director of GEM Estates, offers some insight into the future of Morocco's property prices and the best places to buy.

Prices have been growing steadily for the past three years at a rate of between 15% to 20% per annum, but it is hard to generalise. Quality and square metre sizes are improving and prices will continue to grow at a steady rate for the next few years at least. Some people say that Morocco is expensive and that certain areas of Spain can sometimes be cheaper, but generally they are speaking about the five-star resorts, such as the Mediterrania Saïdia, which offer world-class amenities. These are geared up to be Morocco's Puerto Banús, and consequently, people should compare prices in such resorts with locations such as Puerto Banús rather than the more affordable Murcia region. Prices are set to continue to increase in Marrakesh because of the growth of tourism and flights, while new areas like Mirleft are only just beginning to be discovered, so now is the time to buy and experience the best appreciation rates.

Risks

There are always risks involved when purchasing abroad – or even in the UK market – although in Morocco these are fairly limited. The first thing to be aware of is that Morocco does have a problem with titles. This won't affect you if you are looking to purchase a newly built property which will have a clean title and municipal backing. However, if you are looking to buy a riad to renovate that may have been in the family for 100 years, you will need to ensure the title is clean, and that all owners – and there may be several – have consented to the sale.

Many people have questioned how safe it is to buy in an Islamic country, and if terrorism is a threat. It is impossible to rule out the potential for terrorist activity in an Islamic country – or indeed any country – but Morocco is one of the safest and least threatening Islamic countries in the world, and certainly more stable than many other investment hotspots, such as Egypt or Turkey.

As for the local reaction to an influx of foreign investment, there will always be a certain level of resentment towards foreign investors who are coming in, buying up property and pushing up prices – it's inevitable. However, careful planning and a sensible government policy will highlight to the local population the advantages that such investment will bring, such as economic growth, jobs and a higher standard of living. What's more, the Moroccan King has foreseen the potential impact on housing prices that this influx will cause, and consequently he has committed to a social housing policy that will allow the locals to continue to afford property. Developments offer property at €20,000, along with special financing packages to avoid the wealth divide growing exponentially, especially as Morocco already has a problem with poverty. While politically the country is stable, there have been problems with corruption, although again noises have been made about this and action taken to try to eliminate these problems. Either way, this shouldn't impact on the investor or second-home buyer.

51

Finally, some people have questioned – as with Dubai – the possibility of the government rescinding the right of foreigners to purchase and own homes in the country. This is unlikely to happen, and while you can never second-guess a government, given that Morocco has rebuilt its economy based on tourism and foreign investment, it seems extremely unlikely to occur – bear in mind that Morocco receives more foreign investment than any other Middle Eastern or African country.

MOROCCO'S REGIONS

Chaouia-Ouardigha

Location: North-central Morocco
Area: 7,010 sq km
Population: 1.65 million
Regional capital: Settat
Property hotspots: Benslimane, Settat
Average monthly temperature/rainfall: 22°C/2.4 cm

Bordering Casablanca, Rabat and Marrakesh, this is a fairly unremarkable area which consists of vast, expansive plains, in which lie the three main towns of the area – Benslimane, Settat and Khouribga. Comprising roughly 6% of Morocco's entire population, one third of the populous live in urban areas, with unemployment levels high given the lack of industry. Known for its phosphate production, the Plateau des Phosphates – where the phosphates are intensively mined – is situated to the north of Khouribga, while to the south lies the Zaër-Zaïane forest and in the south west the valley of l'Oum Rbis, an area peppered with lush valleys and impressive gorges. Bordering the Atlantic Ocean, the region can suffer from strong winds and heavy rains.

Benslimane is the main city of note and is known as 'The Green City', since it has no polluting industries, while Settat is a large town and also the centre of the Moroccan cotton industry. There has been new investment in Settat and this can be seen in the recently constructed nine-hole golf course and the civic and commercial architecture of the place. However, this is not really a region which attracts foreigners, other than those passing through to the Atlas Mountains, Marrakesh, Rabat or Casablanca.

Doukkala-Abda

Location: West-central Morocco
Area: 13,285 sq km
Population: 1.98 million
Regional capital: Safi
Property hotspots: Safi, El Jadida, Oualidia, Azemmour
Average monthly temperature/rainfall: 23.2°C/2.1 cm

The coastal region of Doukkala-Abda comprises two provinces, Safi and El Jadida, and occupies part of the popular Atlantic coastal stretch of Morocco, running from just south of Casablanca down to Souira Kedima. The region's 300 km of coastline offers a series of dunes and sandy beaches, while inland it's verdant and lush, comprising the fertile plains of Doukkala and Abda, from which the region takes it name. This area is less densely populated than much of the Atlantic coast and consequently not as prominent on the tourist itinerary. Despite having some of Morocco's most beautiful beaches and interesting history – Safi was the first place to embrace Islam, and there is a strong Portuguese presence throughout the area – many people are ignorant of its charms. This oversight is also exacerbated by the lack of a major international airport, while the region's heavy-duty industry has put many tourists off.

This is an important area in terms of shipping trade, and both Safi and El Jadida are important ports, responsible for 30% of Moroccan exports. Fishing is key to the regional economy, with the towns of Safi and Oualidia important centres of sardine, clam and oyster production. Agriculture is equally important as this is a fertile area,

53

with the ground also rich in mining resources. All in all, this is a vital economic centre within Morocco.

Safi is the regional capital and an important centre of pottery production. Its coastline is called the Yellow Coast, thanks to the yellow-coloured clay which is found here. Not Morocco's most picturesque city – a result of the industry based here – it is still a modern, vibrant place that has an interesting medina and fort.

Oualidia, north of Safi, is popular with northern Moroccan families, who come here for long weekend breaks, but is pretty much unknown by foreigners. This town has a beautiful setting, overlooking a lagoon with a white, sandy beach, while the centre has a certain ancient charm.

The main resort in Doukkala-Abda is El Jadida, which is quite a tourist magnet. It has a stylish and attractive centre, while it also boasts a Blue Flag beach and many restaurants and hotels. The medina is very European in style, thanks to the Portuguese occupation of this area, and you'll find numerous Moroccans from Casablanca, Marrakesh, Fès and Tangier residing here.

Nearby Azemmour is much more introvert. Situated on the mouth of the Oum er Rbia River, it's known for its distinctive embroidery and has an attractive red-walled medina and gorgeous beaches. Its position as a tourist backwater is set to change, as the coastline between Azemmour and El Jadida has been earmarked for re-development under Plan Azur, with some major property developments planned. See page 105 for more details on Plan Azur resorts.

Property focus: The Atlantic coast

The Atlantic Coast has been earmarked as one of the major locations for development as part of the forward-thinking Plan Azur. Located close to the town of El Jadida is the £3.3 million resort of Mazagan, situated on the beachfront, which will offer a

600-bed hotel, restaurants, a casino, an 18-hole golf course and a number of private residences. The resort, along with the development of a new and improved infrastructure, is helping to develop the blossoming tourist industry here, and also encourage investment. The knock-on effect on the surrounding towns is set to be positive, as demand for both second homes and short-term rentals looks set to rise.

El Jadida

There are many bargains still to be had here, but only if you intend to buy soon – this market is on the up. The Portuguese medina of El Jadida is set to undergo a facelift and, once restored, prices will rise as demand grows, especially as back in 2006 a motorway connecting El Jadida with Casablanca was opened. Prices in the medina range from £20,000 (302,928 dirhams) for a renovation project to £50,000 (757,296 dirhams) for a riad in the popular mosque area, or with views over the ramparts. For just £52,200 (790,739 dirhams) you can buy a modern apartment with a living area of 108 square metres.

Given that tourism is on the rise, you can also expect to secure some excellent rental income in the future, especially if you buy a traditional property.

In the Ville Nouvelle, property is modern, although buildings are rarely more than three stories high, given planning restrictions. You'll generally be faced with a choice of apartments or villas and prices range from £30,000 (455,478 dirhams), up to £50,000 (757,296 dirhams) for a three-bedroom villa.

Azemmour

Now that the nearby Mazagan development is nearly completed (see page 105 for details on Plan Azur resorts) the property market in this pretty coastal town has started to expand, and the future looks promising given its proximity to the new resort, golf course,

Casablanca airport and the UNESCO World Heritage site in El Jadida. Unfortunately, Azemmour's medina has fallen into disrepair, but this does give buyers the opportunity for some real bargains for those prepared to renovate – you're looking at less than £20,000 (302,928 dirhams) for a basic property, with modern homes found in the nearby development.

Safi

Unlike the other two towns already mentioned, Safi doesn't hold the same appeal and attractiveness of its neighbours, being more industrial. However, investment is being encouraged via the introduction of low prices, and there are very few planning restrictions imposed on renovations. Officials are keen to transform Safi into a resort mirroring nearby Essaouria, and while there are certainly the leisure and cultural attractions to do so, in terms of facilities and infrastructure, Safi has a long way to go. However, it is earmarked to receive cruise ships in the future, which will help to bolster the tourism infrastructure, and it's situated on the national rail network, making it fairly accessible.

In terms of property, in the medina you can pick up a home to renovate for less than £10,000 (151,996 dirhams) – prices are so low as most are in a very poor state of repair. There are few newly built apartment blocks here and so outside of the medina you are looking at purchasing land (which costs from £10–£40 (152–608 dirhams) per square metre) or villas on the coast (£140,000 (2,128,078 dirhams)).

Fès-Boulemane

Location: northern Morocco
Area: 19,795 sq km
Population: 1.6 million
Regional capital: Fès
Property hotspots: Fès, Sefrou
Average monthly temperature/rainfall: 24°C/2.71 cm

This is one of Morocco's most fertile areas, with 39% of the region covered by forest and 18% used for agriculture. The southern edge of Fès-Boulemane borders the Middle Atlas mountains. Despite being verdant and offering swathes of oak and cedar trees, the majority of the region remains off the tourist radar, with Fès being the main attraction for visitors. However, the regional tourist board is aiming to change this. This area has a stunning landscape, complete with gorges, waterfalls, orchards and lakes, and the rolling hills and dense forests are perfect for skiing, trekking and wildlife opportunities. The unique nature of the landscape here has led many to comment that it is more reminiscent of Europe than Africa – especially noteworthy is the Tazzeka National Park.

Fès is Morocco's third largest city and the beating heart of the region. With 96% of the area's industry located here and two-thirds of the population, it is unsurprising that it is such a magnet for tourists and property investors. There has been much work carried out in and around Fès in 2007, with more than 1,000 new business launched, the construction of a new Fès–Oujda motorway and the restoration of the ancient walls of the city. Under the government's new Plan Azur scheme, Fès's regional tourism body is working towards achieving a capacity of 10,400 beds by 2015, instead of the existing 580 beds, and occupancy is already up to 58% compared with 34% in 2007. Two new tourist zones will be created in the districts of Ouislane and Oued Fès, which will offer over 3,100 beds, and additional accommodation capacity will be created in the medina through the conversion of historical houses and palaces. Fès's other major industry is traditional crafts – this is the centre of Morocco's artisan industry – and there are also aims to increase turnover levels achieved from this industry by 20% to 3.2 million dirhams by 2011. Figures are already up 500% on 2006.

One of Morocco's four imperial cities there is a distinctive French influence in Fès, more obviously in the new town. However, step over into the ancient medina – Fès el Bali – and it feels like you are stepping back in time. Classed as a UNESCO World Heritage site, it's full of wonderful sights, including a mile-long line of souks, the Merenid Tombs, from where you can get a fantastic view of the city, and the old Andalucian quarter. Be prepared to get lost when exploring, as the medina has evolved randomly and the existence of a map is laughable. Nevertheless, part of the charm is simply to explore the nooks and crannies of the whitewashed quarter, which leaves you feeling a million miles away from Western Europe.

The French-created part of the city is known as the Ville Nouvelle, and is now full of towering apartment blocks – this is the place to buy a modern apartment. There is also new Fès – or Fès el Djedid – which was built in the 13th century. Originally designed as a military town, most of the space is taken up by the vast Dar el Makhzen Palace, built as a home to the royal family, and the garrison for the army.

Moving south brings you to the ancient walled city of Sefrou, located 28 km from Fès, in the foothills of the Middle Atlas Mountains. With a population of only 40,000, Sefrou is unknown to foreigners – largely thanks to its proximity to Fès – meaning that property prices and the cost of living remain low, and the well-preserved medina free of tourists and the resulting tat that tends to accompany them. This traditional town actually predates Fès, and its lush surroundings saw it acquire the name Jardin de Maroc. Sefrou could soon develop into a popular location as the more traditional houses are sold at prices that way undercut those asked in Fès. As more and more people start exploring the market, Sefrou is one to watch.

Property focus: Fès

Known as the Florence of Morocco, the fabulous city of Fès is a stunningly beautiful and historic centre, which has been designated a UNESCO World Heritage site.

The market here is hot at the moment, especially as you can now fly direct from the UK with Ryanair, and accessibility is one of the key reasons why the market has taken off. Fès abounds in traditional riads which are currently much cheaper than in Marrakesh and a four-bedroom riad with numerous architectural features and a patio with a fountain can be purchased for a mere £149,000 (2,268,587 dirhams). With the advent of direct flights from Britain to Fès, bargain prices such as these seem unlikely to last for long, with news of the market spreading and buyers already arriving from Britain, France and America in their droves, all competing to scoop up the bargains before prices match those of Marrakesh – homes here are currently around 50% cheaper. Whereas once a property would take months to shift, today it can be sold in days, with the traditional riads and dars being the most sought after. While prices had tended to remain static despite massive hikes in Marrakesh and Essaouira, they're now appreciating by around 20% to 30% every six months.

What makes Fès so special is the palatial architecture of the riads and dars, which offer sculpted plaster, painted woodwork, wood-clad ceilings, tiled floors and sprawling gardens. The infrastructure and amenities are also being improved, with more bars, restaurants, cafes and shops being introduced into the city.

The majority of properties here do require renovation, so be prepared to put in a lot of time and elbow grease to get your property completed. Currently, the resale market is fairly non-existent as under the rule of the French, Fès was abandoned by many, leaving the city to fall into disrepair. Consequently, as there are few habitable properties in the city, so the likelihood is that the resales market will expand massively over the next few years. Prices here start from around £15,000 to £20,000 (228,463 to 304,618 dirhams) and are currently increasing at around 30% a year, although be aware that as well as being faced with a wealth of restoration headaches, many of these properties will lack a title, which is one of the main problems facing the property industry in Morocco.

59

Prices in the medina vary depending on location. The further away from the gates of the medina, the lower the cost. Newer properties can be found in Batha and Zitoun, which are closer to the walls, while there are large houses to purchase in Rcif. Talla Sghir and Talla Kabira are the busiest parts of the medina and the main throughfares. Demand is high here, and consequently premiums are paid on properties – generally, you are looking at between £20,000 and £100,000 (304,618 and 1,524,284 dirhams) depending on the location, size and condition of the property. On the outskirts of the medina you'll find the neighbourhoods of Batha and Ziat, the equivalent of Beverley Hills, where homes are large, modern and expensive.

If you are looking to buy in the new town (Ville Nouvelle), expect to be looking at newly built apartments, which will cost between £20,000 and £40,000 (304,618 and 609,713 dirhams) for two bedrooms, depending on location and amenities.

Gharb-Chrarda-Béni Hssen

Location: North-west Morocco
Area: 8,805 sq km
Population: 1.9 million
Regional capital: Kenitra
Property hotspots: Kenitra
Average monthly temperature/rainfall: 22°C/4.1 cm

One of Morocco's smallest regions, yet boasting a population of 1.9 million people, this area relies heavily on agriculture, with farming the primary industry, employing 68% of the populous. Running adjacent to the Atlantic Ocean, the region is situated close to Rabat, and is well located for access to Casablanca, Tangiers and Fès. It comprises two provinces, those of Kenitra and Sidi Kacem. As with many of Morocco's regions, it is relatively unknown, and largely overlooked – unless you're a birdwatcher. Thanks to the many lakes and estuaries in the region, twitchers regard this as an international hotspot. The Lac de Sidi Bourhaba in particular is home to some rare species, and the Sebou Estuary is also a popular spot. As with many of Morocco's regions, Gharb-Chrarda-Béni Hssen is a surprisingly green area, with 1,250 sq km of forest, which is roughly one-seventh of the entire region.

The main focus of this area is the port of Kenitra, which was established by the French in order to channel trade from Fès and Meknès – an aim that failed thanks to the development of Casablanca and Tangier. It is situated on the Sebou River and nearby is Plage Mehdiya, a long stretch of beach popular with local tourists which is overlooked by Mehdiya village and the ruins of the local kasbah. Today the city is home to 300,000 people, most of whom are employed in the city's paper mills and fish cannery. This is Morocco's sixth largest port and, while it has an attractive centre, there is little of interest here in cultural terms. Nevertheless, this is a modern city with attractive property prices, many art deco and modern buildings and numerous bars and restaurants – there are few traditional properties though.

Greater Casablanca

Location: North-west Morocco
Area: 1,615 sq km
Population: 3.85 million
Regional capital: Casablanca
Property hotspots: Casablanca, Mohammedia
Average monthly temperature/rainfall: 22°C/2.4 cm

Did you know?

Claim to fame: Casablanca's association with the 1940s classic film of the same name, with Humphrey Bogart and Ingrid Bergman – amazingly, no scenes from the film were shot in the city.

Main site of interest: The Mosque of Hassan II with its 200-metre-high minaret which makes it the tallest structure in the country.

Morocco's most densely populated region, this tiny province consists solely of the city of Casablanca (known as Dar-el-Baida in
Arabic, or Casa to the locals) and its suburbs. A small fishing port
up until the reign of the French Protectorate, today it is a sprawling
metropolis and a cosmopolitan centre, which has more in common
with the European capital cities than Africa – in fact, Casablanca
has been described as having more in common with Marseille than
Morocco. Of the region's 3.8 million population, 3.1 million live in
Casablanca, a city which is a mish mash of cultures, architecture and
peoples.

This modern, lively city is the economic capital of Morocco, its chief
port and the sixth largest city on the African continent. Most of
Morocco's modern industries are based here and it contributes 54%
of the country's industrial production, uses 35% of its electricity and
employs 40% of Morocco's workforce. The city is also a transport
hub, with many international flights landing here, and there are
good road and train networks connecting you to the rest of the
country.

As with many destinations in Morocco, Casablanca is working hard
to improve its tourist figures and international appeal. Investment is
soundly encouraged and electronics and telecommunications are two
growing industries – Casablanca is already home to the headquarters
of all the major banks. The aim is to attract one million tourists per
year by 2012, and Casablanca looks like it is a sound investment
opportunity.

While there are some sights to see – such as the Hassan II Mosque,
the second largest mosque in the world – the city is marked primarily
by French influences, and is modern in nature. Once you leave
Casablanca, you'll come across the *bidonvilles* (shanty towns), the
result of many Moroccans being drawn to the economic capital to
find work, while the city itself is surrounded by the drab Chaouia
Plains. Consequently, the exotic image of Casablanca as a romantic
film set location simply isn't accurate – despite the iconic movie of

the 1940s, starring Humphrey Bogart and Ingrid Bergman, being named after the city, not a single shot from the film was actually filmed there.

In Greater Casablanca there is little between the two cities of Casablanca and Rabat other than scruffy, wooded landscape, and few urban centres, other than that of Mohammedia. Serving the dual purpose of being an industrial and commercial centre – Mohammedia is the site of Morocco's largest oil refineries – the city is also a resort and holiday destination for Casablanca's residents. Only 15 miles north of Casablanca, Mohammedia is home to around 200,000 Moroccans and was originally called Fedala, being renamed after the death of King Mohammad V. It offers one of the finest beaches on the Atlantic coastline, a racecourse, marina and golf club. The city keeps its two distinct halves very separate, and consequently this has become an affluent resort. Most of the tourists here are Moroccan, with foreigners preferring the resorts further south. However, this is an attractive destination with a fine array of hotels and restaurants that will appeal to many Europeans.

Property focus: Casablanca

When asked about the market in Casablanca, many agents simply say, 'Watch this space.' The government has promised that over the next few years, Morocco's commercial capital will transform from being a polluted, overcrowded metropolis into a cultural tourist destination, in a similar vein to the investment in Tangier. The city is aiming to attract one million tourists by 2010 – predominantly weekend city breakers – and consequently the run-down areas are being given a facelift, especially the beachfront. The city has been described as lacking culture – in fact, there are no museums or theatres here – but things are beginning to change.

However, Casablanca has a long way to go before becoming a destination for second-home buyers, and the majority of foreigners who purchase here do so as they have relocated for work purposes. The second most expensive city after Marrakesh, largely due to the fact that many Moroccans live and work here, the most expensive places to buy are in the zones around Racine, Boulevard d'Anfa and Al Massira, known as the golden triangle. Most available property in these areas are apartments and duplexes which range in price from £90,000 (1,368,230 dirhams) for a two-bedroom apartment to £400,000 (6,081,024 dirhams) for a four- to five-bedroom duplex. However, you can also find renovation projects, plus houses and villas for resale. Other areas include the up-and-coming Roche Noire near the port, where property would set you back by an average of £275 (4,181 dirhams) per square metre, while for villas, you're looking at Quartier Californie, Anfa and the roads out to Marrakesh and El Jadida. Prices vary drastically and can range from £180,000 (2,736,686 dirhams) to upwards of £900,000 (13,683,659). There are also increasing numbers of developments springing up in this area, such as the Sunset Beach club on the Route d'Azemmour. Incorporating a private beach and eight communal swimming pools, prices start from £73,858 (1,122,941 dirhams) for a fully furnished and air-conditioned apartment, rising to £324,701 (4,917,295 dirhams) for a four-bedroom, four-bathroom villa.

Jet to let prospects in the city are good as there tends to be a shortage of short-term rents, yet given Casablanca's position as an economic hub and capital in all but name, there is always demand, especially as increasing numbers of foreign companies set up offices here. This, coupled with the aims to increase visitor numbers, means Casablanca is earmarked for significant growth in the next few years and so investors should look to buy now, before prices go through the roof.

Ten kilometres of coastline around Casablanca has also been earmarked for development, with Dubai-based developers Emaar buying a 530 hectare plot of land at Bahia Bay to build luxury, upmarket homes.

Mohammedia

Just 25 km from Casablanca is Mohammedia, a port and beach resort, which offers three kilometres of sandy beach and sees some seriously expensive yachts docked in its port. While out of season it can feel like something of a ghost town, during the summer months the resort is packed with primarily Moroccans. The town itself is clean and verdant, with palm trees lining every street, and it attracts an affluent clientele, evidenced by the 18-hole golf course, casino, racecourse, sailing opportunities, and the fact that much of its industry lies in oil.

Generally speaking, many of the properties here are purpose-built villas, although land is becoming increasingly scarce and so newly built apartment complexes are also springing up. The area between the Kasbah and the coast tends to see the most demand, and to purchase a two-bedroom apartment here you would be looking at £45,000 (680,912 dirhams), while a villa 100 metres from the beach would set you back £388,264 (5,874,974 dirhams). An important feature of the market is the new development which is set to be constructed on the coastline between Rabat and Mohammedia. Bouznika Bay is one of the areas being developed, and it already offers golfing, plus excellent surfing and windsurfing amenities. The resort itself offers property from a fairly pricey £60,000 (907,922 dirhams), although this development has been designed for the more affluent investor.

Guelmim-Es Semara

Location: Southern Morocco
Area: 122,825 sq km
Population: 462,410
Regional capital: Guelmim
Property hotspots: Guelmim and surrounding villages, Tan Tan, Plage Blanche
Average monthly temperature/rainfall: 21.6°C/0.8mm

Did you know?

This region is known as the Gateway to the Sahara.

Camel is the most commonly eaten meat here, with hedgehog not far behind.

A juxtaposition of arid desert and 200 km of azure ocean – in fact, the Canary Islands lie just off the coast of Guelmim-Es Semara – this is Morocco's largest region and also the Gateway to the Sahara. The southern half of Guelmim-Es Semara actually comprises part of the disputed Western Sahara territory and although sand dunes are lacking, this is harsh, unattractive terrain. However, there are also thermal springs and lush oases in parts of the region, with the villages surrounding Guelmim offering some attractive properties. Travel away from the interior and you will find yourself on a stunning tract of coastline, consisting of sandy dunes and endless miles of white sand – generally speaking, this area has been inhabited by nomads for the better part of its existence.

The regional capital of Guelmim is a rather drab affair. Once a city of lawlessness, today it has little to recommend it other than its weekly souk and the week-long camel fair held during the summer months. Despite many government attempts to encourage tourism and investment into this region, it still feels fairly cut off from the rest of the country.

However, this is all set to change as the resort of Plage Blanche, with its 50 km of sandy beach, has been earmarked for development by Spanish company Fadesa. Their proposed resort includes hotels and holiday villages, as well as leisure facilities, such as a golf course and a shopping centre. Ecotourism will be a central feature, thanks to the abundance of wildlife here, and the development is expected to be open by 2012. The feeling is that despite the lack of infrastructure and cultural sights that many other Moroccan regions offer, this development will attract tourists thanks to its amenities, high standard of finishing and the stunning Atlantic coastline.

Continue south and you'll come to another proposed tourism site, that of Tan Tan Plage (El Ouatia). Supposedly earmarked for development, plans have been abandoned, and it remains fairly isolated and devoid of tourists, despite many efforts to transform it into an investment hotspot. Currently, fishing, swimming and surfing are the main pastimes, with the town of Tan Tan itself 28 km away. Tan Tan is a centre for fishing and sardine exports, although the government has been offering land packages to investors at low prices in an attempt to revitalise the area. Consequently, this could eventually become a popular location, although at present it feels fairly isolated.

Laâyoune-Boujdour-Sakia El Hamra

Location: Southern Morocco
Area: 139,480 sq km
Population: 256,152
Regional capital: Laâyoune (El Aaiún)
Property hotspots: Laâyoune
Average monthly temperature/rainfall: 24°C/0.72

Did you know?
The regional capital Laâyoune is home to two-thirds of the areas population.

This is one of Morocco's least populated regions, and together with Oued Eddahab-Lagouira, is known as the Western Sahara region. This is currently a disputed territory with its future yet to be ruled on by the World Court. Previously a Spanish colony, today the Moroccan people consider this area as part of their country, although technically the Western Sahara is a self-governing territory. The region's 'ownership' is currently being disputed between the rebel Polisario Front independence movement and the Kingdom of Morocco.

Geographically, it mainly consists of desert flatlands and is the most sparsely populated region in Africa, as well as Morocco. The main conurbation is Laâyoune, home to 200,000 people and the majority of the region's population. Only founded in the 1940s, it is the main driving force behind the Western Sahara economy and has been the subject of a major cash injection from the Moroccan government. A pleasant place, there is evidence of the previous Spanish occupation seen by a smattering of street signs, the old cathedral and the dishevelled Spanish settlement in the city's south. Located close to the coast, there is excellent windsurfing to be had thanks to the strong winds which ravage the coastline and, outside of Laâyoune, most of the inhabitants are fishermen. Within the town itself, government initiatives have made the residents fairly wealthy, and consequently property – which tends to consist of newly built apartments – is pricey.

The positives aside, despite the promise of tax-free living, double wages and subsidised land in the Saharan regions, there are many negatives that you need to be aware of. For one thing, this is a heavily militarised zone as well as being a disputed territory. It is also extremely isolated and despite Laâyoune's size, it sits smack in the middle of the desert, 700 km from Morocco-proper. Tourism is minimal here and although it is now easy to get about – there are flights from Casablanca and Agadir into Laâyoune – and land is heavily subsidised, you should think carefully before investing here.

Marrakesh-Tensift-El Haouz

Location: North-west Morocco
Area: 31,160 sq km
Population 3,102,652
Regional capital: Marrakesh
Property hotspots: Marrakesh, Essaouira
Average monthly temperature/rainfall: 27°C/1.3

Did you know?

Claim to fame: Marrakesh has the largest souk in Morocco, and the busiest and most fascinating city square in the whole of Africa, Djemaa el Fna.

Main site of interest: The medina of Marrakesh, where you'll find Djemaa el Fna and the Koutoubia minaret, the symbol of Morocco.

The region of Marrakesh-Tensift-El Haouz is home to Morocco's most famous city, Marrakesh, which is the focal point for much of the tourism and property investment in the country, with a staggering one-third of all visitors heading here. The central region of Marrakesh-Tensift-El Haouz borders the High Atlas to the south and the waters of the Atlantic to the west. One-third of the regional population live in urban areas, with two million residing in Marrakesh alone.

Marrakesh is the second largest city in Morocco after Casablanca and has always been a colourful centre of trade, entertainment and culture. Think of Morocco and automatically people think of the red-walled splendour of Marrakesh's medina, which to many international visitors typifies the country. The origins of the city are Berber rather than Arabic, with Marrakesh being constructed as the new capital back in the 11th century by the Almoravid tribe. However, despite being over 900 years old, today Marrakesh is a modern and affluent centre, home to some of Morocco's wealthiest and most glamorous citizens, and boasting many chic restaurants and international boutiques. Athough the investment that has been pouring into Marrakesh has made it one of Africa's most opulent cities, which in turn has helped to improve living standards, this has come at a price, with residents subjected to rising levels of pollution, and poverty and wealth found in equal measure. Offering an extremely European feel thanks to the multicultural bars, restaurants, cinemas, shops, supermarkets, opera house and art gallery, many have labelled Marrakesh as the 'St Tropez of the Maghreb', and today the city is home to some of the world's finest houses, palaces, gardens and architecture, which have in turn inspired numerous authors, artists, writers and films.

A verdant place, Marrakesh has many stunning homes and some fabulous gardens, including the botanic gardens of Majorelle, the 12th-century Agdal gardens, and the Saadian pavilion and olive groves of Menara. Set against the backdrop of the Atlas Mountains, it's a picturesque centre that's full of warm and welcoming people, as well as being home to the continent's busiest square, Djemaa el Fna. The ski slopes of the Atlas Mountains, only 80 km away, have added to the appeal for investors.

As with Fès, Marrakesh is divided into two separate districts: the Medina and the Villa Nouvelle, or new town. Marrakesh's medina is red in colour, and its rose-tinted hue has led to the city being aptly named the 'Red City'. Rebuilt in the 12th century, the medina is surrounded by ten kilometres of walls which contain 20 gates and a sprawling labyrinth of souks, all of which lie to the north of the main square, Djemaa el Fna – which literally means Place of the Dead, due to the fact that public executions were once carried out there. By day, Djemaa el Fna is a bustling market, full of snake charmers and storytellers, but at night it really comes to life with street vendors selling aromatic foods, and musicians and acrobats entertaining the numerous passersby.

The following souks can be found in the medina:

◆ Souk Cherratin: Leather

◆ Souk Haddadine: Blacksmiths

◆ Souk Chouari: Carpenters

◆ Souk des Babouches: Slipper makers

◆ Souk Teinturiers: Dyers

◆ Souk des Bijoutiers: Jewellery

◆ Souk des Chaudronniers: Coppersmiths

◆ Le Criée Berbère: Carpets

- Souk Btana: Sheepskins
- Souk Larzal: Wool
- Souk Marine: Textiles
- Potters Souk: Pottery

Travel south west down the N8 from Marrakesh and you'll find yourself at the hugely popular resort town of Essaouira, also known as Mogador. A picture postcard coastal resort, Essaouira has been occupied since prehistoric times and today its whitewashed medina – complete with turrets and rampart walls – remains virtually intact and has been designated as a UNESCO World Heritage site. With a labyrinth of streets, tiny squares and numerous artisan workshops, this is the most popular resort on Morocco's Atlantic coast, and is also an important and industrious harbour. Over the centuries, Essaouira has been a bustling centre of trade, attracting peoples from all over the world – until the French occupied Morocco and trade was transferred to the northern ports.

Thanks to the *alizee*, a prominent wind that blows throughout the year, this is also an excellent centre for windsurfing. The port is located to the south west of the medina, while just off the coast is the island of Ile de Mogador, home to an abandoned prison, a mosque and some major fortifications – it is also a sanctuary for falcons. Essaouira offers ten kilometres of beachfront, making it popular with tourists, but this has also been a haven for artists, actors and musicians, including Orson Welles, who famously filmed *Othello* here, Jimi Hendrix and Ridley Scott.

As the area around Essaouira has been named as one of the six regions for development under Plan Azur, and due to its current popularity with foreign tourists, the city has attracted investors for some years now, although the extensive development plans are likely to considerably boast tourism and interest.

Property focus: Marrakesh

Exotic, accessible and beautiful, this ochre-coloured city – known as the 'red city' – is the most popular visitor attraction in Morocco, and epitomises the romance and magic of the country. With many cultural attractions, such as museums, art galleries and the opera house, the city also offers many practical facilities, such as international schools, budget flights and supermarkets. Located at the foot of the Atlas Mountains, this has always been the most popular location for foreign buyers, and property prices do reflect this high demand. The city has enjoyed investment totalling a staggering €8 billion (£5.9 billion) over the last year, and the plans for investment include the construction of around 20 new golf courses, luxury hotel resorts, spas, theme parks, water parks and much more, all of which will help draw tourists and investors into the city. The property market is well-established and the French have been buying here for about a decade now – again, this has impacted on the affordability of the city, as well as the availability of the most highly sought after properties: riads to renovate.

Generally, buyers have been drawn by the riads in the medina areas, although there are increasing numbers of newly built properties available and, generally speaking, you'll be able to find everything from city centre apartments and luxury villas to a more traditional riad or plot of land. Marrakesh is a mecca for lovers of traditional properties, with stunning, furnished, two-bedroom, two-bathroom riads in the medina, with superb views, available for £208,000 (3,161,639 dirhams). A two-bedroom apartment in a five-storey block of off-plan apartments with breathtaking views of the Atlas Mountains is available from just £157,444 (2,390,227 dirhams).

There are a number of areas in which to buy and the most popular is within the medina. However, the outskirts of the city are becoming an increasingly sound – and popular – investment. Unlike central Marrakesh, prices on the outskirts aren't as stable as those of the more established urban market, and they can vary dramatically. There are also issues of land ownership, and foreign buyers need to be careful what agreements they enter into, researching what they can and can't buy (see the section on buying land in Chapter 2).

The medina

Marrakesh's medina boasts some of the most expensive property in the whole of Morocco, which is unsurprising given that the demand for homes here is higher than anywhere else in the country. The property market in Marrakesh is driven by European demand, and many investors are buying renovated riads and dars that were previously owned and restored by foreign buyers. The medina has always been the country's biggest draw for property buyers, and a staggering 30% of the 12,000 properties in the old town are now owned by foreigners. Despite the high demand, it is still possible to buy an unrestored house for less than £100,000 (1,517,494 dirhams), but be aware that renovating here is expensive as materials are in short supply. Consequently, those people who have bought and renovated a traditional property will find that the resales market for such homes is thriving, as there are few foreigners buying in Morocco who want the hassle of renovating in a foreign country. A restored riad can be sold for anything from £50,000 to £300,000 (758,747 to 4,552,483 dirhams), depending on the location.

The medina itself has many different areas, and among the more popular locations are those close to the Djemma el Fna, in places such as Mouassine, Kssour and Zitoun, where renovated riads can be picked up for around £40,000 to £60,000 (606,994 to 910,491 dirhams). The areas around the Royal Palace are leafy, quiet and secure, and the roads are wide enough to take cars. Property here is more expensive though, and you're looking at around £250,000 (3,793,713 dirhams) for a large house. A cheaper area is Kinnaria, a quiet neighbourhood in the centre of the medina where you can pick up a riad for between £30,000 to £60,000 (455,245 to 910,491 dirhams).

73

Ville Nouvelle

Where you once would have seen sprawling old houses, today there are newly built apartment blocks. Unfortunately, most of the characterful colonial buildings have been torn down, and those that remain tend to be very costly. Apartments here are popular with affluent Moroccans from the northern cities such as Casablanca, and these blocks are well located close to shops and amenities, and most come with a swimming pool, gardens, concierge, air conditioning and spa facilities – of course, these are more expensive than your average modern apartment. No apartment block can be taller than five storeys, and some are only two storeys high, reminiscent of the days when the limit was set that low.

In Gueliz and Hivernage, you can pick up a one-bedroom apartment from £45,000 to £90,000 (682,813 to 1,365,627 dirhams), rising to £120,000 to £150,000 (1,820,837 to 2,278,078 dirhams) for three bedrooms. Many are owned by the locals who work in Marrakesh, as well as Moroccans from the northern cities who use Marrakesh as a weekend retreat. The majority of buyers tend to use these properties as weekend retreats, although the quieter and more upmarket suburb of Hivernage is a popular retirement location among European buyers.

The suburbs

The suburbs on the outskirts of Marrakesh are becoming increasingly popular as prices continue to go up in the medina and new town. This is further encouraged by the continued development of self-contained communities on the outskirts of the city. Most of the suburban areas have also become more popular thanks to the extension of Avenue Mohammed VI which makes it easier to enter the city centre from the suburbs.

Palmeraie

The nicest and most well-known neighbourhood is **Palmeraie**, ten kilometres to the north of the city, which is situated on the road to

Fès with views of the Atlas Mountains. Home to the rich and famous of Marrakesh, this neighbourhood is known as Millionaire's Row and is full of luxurious red brick villas and a staggering 180,000 palm trees. Many investors buy land and build their own homes here, although regulations are very strict and cutting down one of the sacred palms will land you in prison. You are also required to buy at least one hectare of land if you intend to build here. Different parts of Palmeraie are zoned for different building usages and so space can be scarce, with 146 hectares given over to villas covering 200 square metres plus, 2,300 hectares for reforestation on which building is forbidden, 3,300 hectares for villas of 2,000 to 10,000 sq m and 17 hectares for apartments and duplex developments.

If you're looking to buy a luxury villa you can pay up to three times as much as you would for a property in the medina, with prices starting at £600,000 (9,125,399 dirhams). Apartments can be purchased for around £90,000 (1,368,809 dirhams). A recently finished resort is that of Le Clos de la Palmeraie, a luxurious gated community of 30 modern riads, which start from £110,398 (1,679,043 dirhams) for an apartment. Nearby are a couple of exclusive developments, such as the Palmeraie Golf Palace and Resort, which offers an 18-hole golf course, swimming pools, tennis courts, stables, a club house and luxury hotel and spa facilities. Club Med Village is also situated nearby, which boasts a spa and wellness centre, leisure and sports facilities and a luxury hotel.

Route de L'Ourika

Other popular spots include the **Route de L'Ourika** south of the city, which is one of the most popular places to buy land outside of Marrakesh – although it is not permitted along the first seven kilometres. The road stretches from Marrakesh up to the valley of Ourika, 40 km from the city and, as demand and interest in the area increase, hotels, bars and restaurants have begun to spring up along the route. A lush stretch which is surrounded by countryside and plant nurseries, this is a popular area with developers and developments, especially as you can enjoy views of the Atlas Mountains.

It is possible to buy a 10,506 square metre plot of land for £116,512 (1,900,000 dirhams), but prices for villas vary dramatically – in some instances, a newly built four-bedroom villa can set you back by up to £919,941 (15,000,000 dirhams), while it is also possible to buy a newly built five-bedroom house for £410,127 (6,300,000 dirhams). The average cost of land here hovers at around £62,000 (938,496 dirhams) per hectare, depending on your proximity to Marrakesh.

Route d'Amizmiz

Route d'Amizmiz – also referred to as Route du Barrage – is another attractive route out of Morocco. It leads towards Amizmiz, a small Berber settlement 50 km away from Marrakesh, and the man-made Lake Takerkoust, which supplies much of the city's water. Quieter than the other routes, thanks to the extension of Avenue Mohammed VI it has seen an upturn in demand and construction, and while being easily accessible to Marrakesh's centre, travel just four miles out of town and you'll find yourself in lush countryside, full of olive trees and palms. The first three miles of Route d'Amizmiz takes you through the Agdal area, the Royal Equestrian Club and the Oasiria water park. On this stretch you will find Samanah Country Club, where you can purchase a newly built villa from between £257,740 to £1.4 million (3,901,422 to 21,191,864 dirhams).

Route de Ouarzazate

The **Route de Ouarzazate** is a cheaper area to buy in, thanks to its lack of direct access into Marrakesh and its arid landscape. You can buy a minimum of one hectare of land here, and an eight-hectare plot will set you back by around £307,194 (5,000,000 dirhams), with the average plot costing £20,000 (302,689 dirhams) per hectare. Lying to the east of the city, accessibility isn't as good as the other routes. However, on the plus side this is where you'll find Marrakesh's American school, along with the Royal Golf Course and a luxury hotel. You can buy a house with a living area of 140 square metres and a pool for £169,296 (2,561,913 dirhams) here.

Route de Fès

Finally, **Route de Fès** also lies to the east of Marrakesh, although it's more fertile than the Route de Ouarzazate, with plenty of palm trees. As its name suggests, this stretch of road leads to Fès, and it can be very busy. Other problems include access to Marrakesh, which is not direct given the road's location to the city's east.

This has long been a magnet for the monied Europeans looking for a luxurious villa, and so there are many luxurious hotels and resorts in the area. Land here sells for slightly more than in many of the other suburbs, and the market is more stable here too. A five-hectare plot with olive trees will cost around £307,194 (5,000,000 dirhams) and one hectare around £92,171 (1,500,000 dirhams). A villa estate with 9,000 square metres of land and a guest house will cost from between £596,734 to £969,507 (9,033,703 to 14,676,956 dirhams).

In all cases, the local government has put a halt on the building of any large developments on Marrakesh's outskirts due to limited water supplies, but small parcels of land can still be bought to build individual homes on. If applying for planning permission, always be aware of the zoning restrictions for the area, and stick with the approved plans.

Insider info
Adam Cornwell at GEM Estates offers some advice on buying a home in Marrakesh.

Before considering buying a property in Morocco, one should research the different regions and where better to start than Marrakesh, the cultural capital of the country. Marrakesh is virtually unchanged since the Middle Ages, yet remains perpetually cool and is currently the place to be seen and, indeed, to buy in. The vibrant Djemaa el Fna Square is the heartbeat of the medina, with its labyrinth of streets. Djemaa el Fna throngs with market traders, witchdoctors, musicians and storytellers, all of whom are fighting noisily for the attention of the crowd. Peaceful Hammams, the Moroccan version of a Turkish bath, provide the perfect antidote to the bustle of the medina, whilst chic clubs, restaurants and boutique hotels welcome the well-heeled in their droves. Unfortunately, buying up and renovating an old riad is now old news. If you are looking to buy property in Marrakesh then you would be best advised to look at the up and coming suburbs surrounding Marrakesh.

Property focus: Essaouira

The coastal resort of Essaouira is one of the most popular locations in Morocco with tourists and represents the largest property marker for foreign buyers outside of Marrakesh. This is surprising really, given that the airport is two hours away and there is little of cultural importance here. However, thanks to its expansive sandy beaches and whitewashed medina, coupled with the relaxed and friendly atmosphere the town boasts, this has become an extremely popular centre. An attractive place, everything is accessible on foot and there are numerous cafes, restaurants and amenities to hand.

Most notably, Essaouria has been earmarked as one of the six resorts to be developed under Vision 2010 plans. Due to be completed this year, the new Station Balnéaire de Mogador resort will offer 525 luxury villas, 32 hotels, two golf courses, a spa, cafes, gardens and a beach club. The development will be situated four kilometres outside of Essaouria and will cover an area of 356 hectares. While of course offering a boost to the local economy and tourism in the area, no one is certain what impact this will have on the property market in the medina, although some estate agents believe it will result in soaring prices rather than drawing attention away from Essaouira's centre.

The medina is a UNESCO World Heritage site, so obviously if you are looking to buy to renovate, be aware that there will be planning restrictions. Most properties adhere to the traditional colours of white stonework and blue shutters, and typically are furnished with items made from the local *thuya* wood, with ironwork and pink and yellow sandstone featuring heavily. If you are looking to buy and renovate here, be aware that as this is a small town and many are buying with restoration in mind, local artisans and builders are in short supply.

Around 20% of the 16,000 homes are already in foreign hands, but demand for property continues to be high and consequently prices are rivalling – and in some cases topping – those of Marrakesh. Thanks to the shortage of homes given the small nature of the medina, and the premium location of being on the coast, it can be expensive to buy here. The market is being further fuelled by the introduction of international flights into the local airport, making the prognosis for Essaouira very healthy indeed.

The Medina

The medina is small and so most properties are similar in terms of style, price and attractiveness. Prices are at their highest around the tourist areas of the Kasbah, Bab Sba and the Sqala, which are closer to the sea and offer larger, European-style homes. For a habitable property, expect to pay at least £150,000 (2,269,757 dirhams). Further into the medina, around the residential areas of the Mellah – which is currently undergoing a facelift – and Bab, prices are lower, with a restoration project averaging around £100,000 (1,513,171 dirhams). The less popular areas of Chbanat and Bouakhar in the west are also becoming scrutinised as people look for more affordable options – being further from the sea, salt erosion is also less of a problem, which can also be a plus point. Generally speaking, most properties will set you back by less than £200,000 (3,026,343 dirhams), and for a two-bedroom riad to renovate, complete with courtyard, terrace and connected water and electricity, you're looking at £71,618 (1,083,856 dirhams).

Just outside the medina is Bab Doukkala, which marks the start of the new town. Here, recently built apartment blocks offer two-bedroom properties for around £30,000 (454,015).

> **Top tip**
> As this is a coastal area, sea salt and humidity can damage the exterior of a property, causing paint to peel and metal to rust. Be aware, and take precautions if installing ironwork.

The suburbs

Like Marrakesh, much of the countryside around Essaouira has become popular among foreign buyers, with many plots of land currently for sale. However, given that much of this is agricultural land, you may well need to obtain a VNA (Vocation Non-Agricole) permit, which allows foreigners to purchase agricultural land. See Chapter 5 on purchasing property for more details.

Ghazoua is eight kilometres from Essaouira, and offers traditional stone-built houses, while the tranquil town of **Ounara** is only 20 km away. Both are growing in popularity among foreign buyers, with infrastructure improvements underway to make the main road passable. Small houses with some land can be purchased for as little as £80,000 (1,210,179 dirhams), although they will need modernising. Land is the other option, and prices have recently risen to around £50 (756 dirhams) per square metre, while for £156,700 (2,370,377 dirhams) you can purchase a 6,000 square metre plot in the centre of Ghazoua.

Other areas include **Sidi Kaouki**, Morocco's top beach for surfers and windsurfers. This area gets wind-blasted and there are few properties on the beachfront. However, land here costs as little as £20,000 (302,537 dirhams) a hectare, with renovation properties in the area available for between £20,000 to £30,000 (302,537 to 453,838 dirhams).

Route de Safi, **Route d'Agadir** and **Route de Marrakesh** all run out of Essaouira and have become potential locations for investors to purchase land or maybe a run-down farmhouse. The coast road to Safi is pretty and verdant, with trees and flowers lining the route. Prices vary, with around £193,995 (2,934,748 dirhams) securing you a 37,000 square metre plot, or £110,000 (1,663,969 dirhams) buying you a hectare of land complete with a rustic property. Route d'Agadir is the most scenic, boasting stunning views of the coast and low prices – a ruined farmhouse with land can be bought for as little as £30,000 (453,809 dirhams), while an 11-hectare plot of land would set you back £1,268,644 (19,191,981 dirhams).

Finally the rather bland and arid road to Marrakesh may be unexciting, but travel off-road and you can find some pleasant properties and low prices – just £60,000 (910,917 dirhams) for a farmhouse and a one-hectare plot.

Just on the outskirts of Essaouira is a town called Diabat, made famous following a visit by Jimi Hendrix in the 1960s. It's here that another of the government-backed Plan Azur developments will be built, which will incorporate high-quality hotels, golf courses, a spa centre, property developments, restaurants, bars and gardens. Nearby, the Mogador resort is also being constructed – see page 105 for more details on Plan Azur resorts.

Meknès-Tafilalet

Location: North-central Morocco
Area: 79,210 sq km
Population: 2,141,527
Regional capital: Meknès
Property hotspots: Meknès, Ifrane, Azrou
Average monthly temperature/rainfall: 23.6°C/2.92 cm

> **Did you know?**
> This region is home to the resort of Ifrane, nicknamed Little Switzerland, which is a
> town and ski resort in the Middle Atlas region where you could easily be forgiven
> for thinking you were in the Alps.

Stretching from Meknès in the west, across the country to the border with Algeria, the region of Meknès-Tafilalet is one of the country's largest and also one of the most diverse. To the west lie the agricultural plains of verdant Meknès, to the south are the arid deserts inhabited by the indigenous Berbers, and in between lie the snowy peaks and lush forests of the Middle and High Atlas. Despite its size, this is a sparsely populated area, with nearly 80% of land given over to agriculture. Consequently, tourist amenities are limited and few tourists venture here, despite the epic grandeur of the area – this is Morocco's least visited region. However ecotourism is on the rise, although most people simply come to stay in Meknès, where you'll find the majority of holiday accommodation.

Meknès is the main centre of industry in this region. Home to 536,322 people and situated only 60 km from Fès, it lies in the centre of the Saiss plain, a fertile area packed with olive trees that sits between the Rif and Atlas Mountains. Split into three areas – the Ville Nouvelle, the medina and the largely abandoned Imperial City – Meknès is northern Morocco's main city and is cut in two by the Oued Boufekrane River, with the Ville Nouvelle stretching along the east bank and the medina occupying the west. Moulay Ismael, second ruler of the Moroccan Alaouite dynasty, was responsible for transforming Meknès into the prosperous city it is today. Making it the country's capital back in the 17th century, he built many architectural wonders, with his main achievement being the breath-taking Imperial Palace. While many buildings are now in disrepair, they are thankfully beginning to be restored. Just 33 km to the north lie the ruins of Volubilis, the largest and best-preserved Roman remains in the country.

One of the region's other major towns is Ifrane, nicknamed Little Switzerland. A town and ski resort in the Middle Atlas Mountains, it has a population of 12,000. Lying 50 km from Meknès, you could easily be forgiven for thinking you were in France or Switzerland rather than Morocco, as this is a place built and heavily influenced by the French back in the 1930s, and consequently consisting of ski chalets and boulevards. The Western European nature of the town has led it to be dubbed the 'Geneva of Morocco' and it is frequented by many wealthy Moroccans.

Other places of note include Merzouga, situated on the edge of the Sahara and renowned for its spectacular sand dunes, Azrou and its Kasbah, along with the surrounding market towns of Khenifra and Aïn Leuh and the French outpost of Er Rachidia. None of them are particularly popular with investors, and have few claims to fame, although property prices can be low, and homes spacious.

Property focus: Atlas Mountains and ski resorts

Surprising though it may seem, you can actually ski in Morocco, with the Atlas Mountain resorts of Oukaïmeden – only 50 minutes from Marrakesh – and Mischliffen offering guaranteed ski opportunities from January to April. Estate agents have predicted that over the next 50 years, the more traditional resorts of Europe will lose out to the ski resorts of Africa, and given that Morocco offers an exotic combination of long stretches of sandy beach, golf and watersports facilities, deserts and snow-capped peaks, it has excellent potential as a tourist destination. Currently, homes in the resort are limited, but it is only 50 minutes' drive from Domaine de L'Akhdar in Marrakesh, where Colliers CRE is selling three-bedroom villas, starting from £225,000 (3,413,673 dirhams).

Developer EMAAR has launched a combined golf and ski development, investing $6.8 billion (£3.5 billion) in Morocco. Consequently, the future is looking healthy for its ski resorts. As the market is still underdeveloped and fairly immature, foreigners aren't buying in Morocco specifically for the skiing, but with a new development planned, interest is set to grow.

Ski resorts have been touted as the future of the Moroccan market, with Oukaïmeden tipped to become particularly popular, especially as outside of the skiing season it is a pleasant getaway for nature lovers and outdoor enthusiasts. As a result, developments close to the Atlas Mountains offer excellent investment potential. You can currently buy a one-bedroom apartment in the Atlas Golf from £64,100 (973,462 dirhams), while property at the El Oasis de Marrakesh starts from £80,000 (1,214,969 dirhams).

Oriental

Location: North-eastern Morocco
Area: 82,900 sq km
Population 1.9 million
Regional capital: Oujda
Property hotspots: Saïdia, Oujda, Berkane, Nador
Average monthly temperature/rainfall: 24°C/1.5 cm

Did you know?

Claim to fame: Pilgrims used to leave for Mecca from the oasis town of Figuig.

Main site of interest: Saïdia, with its 20 km of white sandy beaches.

This region stretches from the Mediterranean coast, across the border with Algeria and down to the imperial city of Fès. The landscape is diverse – including forest, mountains, plains, deserts and beaches – and much of the region is unexplored by tourists. The Rif mountain range runs through the area, with the smaller Beni Snassen range an attraction for nature lovers and hikers. The Spanish-held enclave of Melilla is situated on the coast and consequently there is a prevalent Spanish influence in the area largely thanks to the lack of government interest in the region until recently, when the King pledged to redevelop the Oriental. Today it is home to one of the flagship Plan Azur resorts, the Mediterrania Saïdia, which has attracted massive investment into the region. This has had a knock on effect on the fortunes of some of the nearby towns and cities, especially when coupled with the construction of the new Fès-Oujda motorway. While Oriental has historically relied on agriculture and mining, tourism is beginning to play an increasing part in the economy of the region.

The main conurbations in the region include Oujda, a university town which sits on the border with Algeria. Residing on a plain, surrounded by the stunning Beni Snassen Mountains, Oujda has a population of 500,000. It's within easy reach of the coast, mountains and deserts, and is only 14 km from Algeria, although the border between the two countries is often shut thanks to strained relations. Berkane lies between Oujda and Saïdia and is an agricultural town which is bursting with orange trees – in fact, it is the orange capital of eastern Morocco. There isn't much to do in this modern centre, with little in the way of cultural or leisure attractions. However, its proximity to the Saïdia development means that it may well benefit from the inward investment and tourist influx into the region.

Nador is a very Spanish city, only 13 km from the enclave of Melilla, and fairly unremarkable from a tourist perspective, given its industrial nature. However, with Oujda airport set to receive international flights, the new motorway and investment, it won't be long before demand for property skyrockets. Many properties in this town are modern in nature and available for less than £30,000 (456,431 dirhams).

Property focus: Saïdia and Mediterranean coast

This area is seeing some of the most concentrated activity from foreign investors thanks largely to the massive Mediterrania Saïdia resort, one of the first of the government-sponsored Plan Azur resorts to be launched, and one which has been – and continues to be – a phenomenal success. The coastline around Saïdia makes it one of the most appealing stretches of beach in Morocco. With 20 km of white sand and a nearby eucalyptus forest, it was once a quiet summer resort; thanks to Plan Azur, this has all changed.

The Mediterrania Saïdia resort was launched in 2005, and was built by Fadesa, a Spanish developer. Although it won't be complete until 2009, most properties within the development have already been sold. All complexes are built with foreign buyers in mind, as these are self-contained resorts with many amenities onsite. The flagship Mediterrania Saïdia development will cover seven million square metres, offering six kilometres of sandy beach, three 18-hole golf courses, a 750-berth marina, a shopping centre, water parks and a spa and wellness centre. There will also be ten four- or five-star hotels, and numerous boutiques, restaurants and beach clubs, with over 3,000 luxury apartments and villas for sale. Despite all this construction, the aim is to keep 40% of the development a green zone.

Across the resort you can find property ranging from basic one-bedroom apartments to luxury villas – for example, a fully furnished off-plan two-bedroom apartment in Saïdia with views over the golf course and the beach will cost around £156,730 (2,381,468 dirhams), while closer to Tetouan, a similar apartment is priced at £92,778 (1,409,381 dirhams). There are numerous developments within the resort and the most popular are the Jardin de Fleur and Oasis Beach and Golf Resort. In the Sahara Beach and Spa resort, prices start at £80,000 (1,215,577 dirhams) for an apartment, although the average price within the development as a whole for an apartment is £100,000 (1,519,580 dirhams).

Case Study – Investment inspiration

Richard Lee-Smith (35 years) and partner Gemma Mugica Zufiaur (33 years) certainly took a circuitous route to arrive at a property purchase in Le Jardin de Fleur on Morocco's Mediterranean coastline. The couple, who live together in Edinburgh, originally planned for Gemma – a native Spaniard from the city of Vitoria on the northern coastline – to swap her Basque country apartment for a sunnier alternative on the southern Costas.

'Starting with the ubiquitous Google, we set about searching for suitable southern Spanish property but quickly discovered that many agents had diversified into other countries and others had set up as specialist emerging market agencies such as GEM Estates,' explains Richard. 'So I started to research other countries such as Cape Verde, Dubai and Brazil and compared them to Spain. When Morocco popped up on my radar I found the Plan Azur projects backed by the King of Morocco himself very appealing, and the investment potential was clear. And, for somewhere just 14 km from the tip of Spain, the prices were equally alluring. What started as Gemma's project became my adventure and I set up a meeting with GEM Estates, based in Spain, to talk it through further.'

After a long face-to-face chat, Richard, a self-employed IT consultant, took the plunge and reserved a two-bedroom apartment in Les Jardins du Maroc, a beach and golf resort within the Mediterrania Saïdia development. At the time, he took the last available unit and paid in the region of £123,000. Richard looked at other Moroccan resorts for comparison, but with a background in architecture, aesthetics were just as important to him as investment potential, and he felt the distribution, size, specification and facilities of Les Jardins du Maroc were particularly good.

Richard continues, 'A whole raft of elements helped to sway my decision to purchase. Yes, the developer had an excellent track record for design and quality and of course the prices like-for-like with near-neighbour Spain bode well for capital appreciation, but we also looked at the bigger picture. Transportation is vital for a resort's continued success and nearby Oujda Airport is gearing up for the full effects of Open Skies, and ultimately low-cost carriers, by building a new terminal and two new runways. In addition, the link road from Oujda to Mediterrania Saïdia slashes transfer times to 25 minutes, and this is also in its final stages of completion. The King's support is in clear evidence.'

Richard and Gemma plan to use their new apartment for holidays and also to rent it out as part of the optional rental programme, which is tax-free for the first five years. Richard – having been brought up in Carnoustie, an Open Championship venue – will undoubtedly be drawn to the three 18-hole golf courses, while Gemma has the three swimming pools, clubhouse and bar of Les Jardins du Maroc on the doorstep.

When asked to offer advice for would-be purchasers, Richard says, 'We genuinely have found the process to be completely hassle-free thus far. Good communication is a must for me when embarking on a commitment of this scale and GEM Estates has been exemplary in this department. My advice is that the internet is a great place to start information gathering, but only by speaking to the agent will you detect the confidence that they have in their product. Do ask lots of questions, read and research, and Google everything!'

To allay any concerns, Gemma did get a property in southern Spain – she opted for an apartment in Marbella, which was of similar size and specification to the one in Morocco, but at a much higher price!

Oujda

If you are looking for a traditional property – and low prices – then it may be wise to look in the areas surrounding Saïdia, which are benefiting from the investment and influx of tourism that the Mediterrania Saïdia is attracting. Inland is Oujda, the largest city in eastern Morocco and a modern one at that. Surrounded by mountains, the city sits in a plain, and currently there is little demand for property from the overseas market. However, thanks to the city's proximity to the Saïdia development, this is likely to change, especially as many people will begin flying into Oujda airport once the airport upgrade is completed and budget flights arrive. Consequently, while there is little demand for rentals at present, this could be a smart investment, as currently sale prices average around £10,000 to £30,000 (152,097 to 456,291 dirhams) for a traditional property. Oujda has yet to see the introduction of modern apartment blocks so be prepared to modernise any property you buy here.

Berkane

Berkane sits inland from Saïdia, on the main Nador-Oujda road. Surrounded by the Beni-Snassen Mountains, this modern centre is Morocco's orange-producing capital. There is little to do here and the property market is practically non-existent at present – although there are a few developments springing up. However, as with many of the areas in and around Saïdia, Berkane will benefit from the influx of investment and tourism into the region, so watch this space.

You can pick up a habitable house with six rooms for £90,000 (1,368,876 dirhams), while for a four-bedroom house with a courtyard you can expect to pay around £80,000 (1,216,779 dirhams).

Nador

Nearby Nador is a transport hub for ferries arriving from Spain and it also has an airport. Ties between Nador and the neighbouring Spanish enclave of Melilla are very strong – stronger, in fact, than relations with its own Moroccan government. However, the government's plans to develop the Mediterranean coast will positively affect Nador, which has previously suffered from being cut off from the rest of Morocco. There will be a new Tangier–Saïdia road constructed, which will link Nador with the coastline, and more notably, a new rail link will attach Nador to the main Fès–Taourirt line. While this is a relatively uninspiring place, with few traditional or newly built homes, these infrastructure changes, plus proximity to the developed coastline, could well impact on the investability of the centre. A 123 square metre plot of land 15 minutes from the coast will cost around £26,000 (395,062 dirhams), rising to £180,00 (2,737,493 dirhams) for a five-bedroom house, five minutes from the beach.

Case Study – Steve and Cheryl Hubbard

Steve and Cheryl Hubbard travelled to Morocco on a Compass Properties viewing trip in May 2005. The couple from Manchester had done a lot of research on the internet and were attracted by the investment opportunity, golden sandy beaches, the King's ten-year plan, prices starting from £38,000 for a property on the Mediterranean coast, and a location which enjoyed the same climate as Spain.

'After miles of scenery, a tour of the golf club and the Marina, we arrived at the building site of Jawhara Smir, which was surrounded by mountains, with no infrastructure and miles of undeveloped land,' said Steve. 'We started asking ourselves questions – can it work as an investment? Who would want to come here? The alarm bells were sounded but it was too late as the charm of Morocco had already captured us. 'It is now more than two years since we bought our first apartment in Jawhara and we have spent many holidays relaxing by the pool, on the beach, sampling the Moroccan cuisine in the marina restaurants and the culture of the local medina.'

The Hubbards are confident that the holiday season in Morocco will extend beyond July and August. Each time they visit, they notice the changes in building projects and the new infrastructure being put into place to support the tourist market. In May 2007, the couple imported a sports boat to Marina Smir to make the most of the Mediterranean location.

'This has been a success story for us and Compass Properties,' said Steve. 'We look forward to spending more time in this beautiful part of Morocco developing our own business. We want to be here for the start of this inevitable tourist boom.'

Insider info

Steve Burns, Marketing Manager of Compass Properties, offers us some insight into the Costa Vista, a hotspot on Morocco's Mediterranean Coast.

The greatest change in the Moroccan market has been the Mediterranean coast – the Costa Vista. This was largely ignored by the previous King and so is relatively undeveloped, yet offers major advantages to purchasers compared to other Moroccan destinations such as Marrakesh – it is certainly greater value for money. The Mediterranean coast has superb beaches and the climate is more temperate than the Atlantic.

Currently, prices are at a substantial discount compared to other Moroccan destinations and the traditional second-home markets of southern Europe, but are increasing, so the advice would be to move quickly. In early 2007, single-bed hotel-style apartments in Mirador Golf were selling for £23,000. These units quickly sold out due to huge demand. Unprecedented capital growth has seen the value of similar units at Playa Vista starting at £39,500, with only very few remaining available. Meanwhile, two-bedroom apartments in Playa Vista are selling for £64,900, while the recently released Cabo Dream development offers one-bedroom apartments from £48,960, and two-bedrooms from £54,000.

Oued Ed-Dahab-Lagouira

Location: Southern Morocco
Area: 50,880 sq km
Population: 99,367
Regional capital: Dakhla
Property hotspot: Dakhla
Average monthly temperature/rainfall: 24°C/0.72 cm

Did you know?

Oued Ed-Dahab-Lagouira is situated in the disputed territory of the Western Sahara, which Moroccans consider part of their country. The Polisario Front regard this area as part of the Sahrawi Arab Democratic Republic, while the United Nations doesn't recognise either Moroccan sovereignty over the area, nor the self-declared Sahrawi Republic.

This is the least populated of Morocco's regions, with Dakhla home to only 67,468 residents, making it the country's smallest settlement. As it was formerly colonised by the Spanish it has a very Andalucian feel, with whitewashed buildings and a Spanish-style cathedral. During the Spanish Civil War, writer Pedro García Cabrera was held in the prison here, with Franco building one of three paved runways in this area. The government has begun developing this isolated outpost, investing money in an attempt to improve the local industry and infrastructure – there are regular flights into Dakhla's airport from Casablanca and Agadir. While it has been successful in these aims, this does not really detract from the fact that Dakhla is surrounded by vast expanses of desert and is fairly isolated. Today Dakhla is a bustling military outpost, and also home to a thriving octopus and calamari fleet.

Land here is incredibly cheap – as you would expect – and despite the fact that this is a largely military area, the government is still keen to encourage investment. That said there is – unsurprisingly – little, if any demand for property here.

Rabat-Salé-Zemmour-Zaer

Location: North-east Morocco
Area: 9,580 sq km
Population: 2.4 million
Regional capital: Rabat
Property hotspots: Rabat, Salé
Average monthly temperature/rainfall: 22°C/3 cm

Home to Morocco's capital, Rabat, this expansive region is largely uninhabited, with 75% of the 2.4 million populous living in the two major towns of Rabat and Salé. The region touches the Atlantic coast to the west, while inland you'll find numerous forests of cork, fertile plains and fields full of crops.

Despite being the capital, Rabat is certainly not as prodigious or bustling a centre as Marrakesh, Casablanca or Tangier. Pronounced the capital in the 20th century by the French, Morocco's political epicentre certainly isn't at the top of the average visitor's itinerary, and this is unsurprising. While being elegant and European in nature, this is a very quiet city, with many of the eateries and bars shut by 10 pm. That said, the architectural and cultural history is fascinating, with many Arabic and French monuments, as well as beaches and the ancient medina with its souks – Rabat's kasbah is one of the most striking monuments in this city, and its bab (gateway) dates back to the 12th century.

Rabat is situated on the Oued Bou Regreg estuary, with Salé sat on the opposite bank, and it has a small beach that borders the estuary. Salé is pretty much an extension of Rabat these days, and regarded as a suburb of the city that it historically always had pre-eminence over. A port town, today it is shadowed by the success of Casablanca, and despite being modern, with an expanding Ville Novuelle, you can still see the medieval walls and walk the streets of the medina with its busy souks. Within the walls of the medina you'll also find the Grand Mosque and Medersa, both of which are fascinating.

With much redevelopment going on in this area, including the connecting of Salé and Rabat with a tramway, there are great plans for investment and construction around the two centres, with the aim to put Rabat on the tourist and property investment map. Already popular with French retirees, this is one to watch.

Property focus: Rabat and Salé

Morocco's capital city is much overlooked by foreign investors and tourists; that said, this is an area greatly favoured by the French. Situated 70 km north of Casablanca, few airlines actually fly directly into Rabat, which has hindered its development. Contrary to what many think, this is actually a pretty place, with a relaxed atmosphere, wide, attractive boulevards and many cultural and leisure pursuits. Large numbers of French retirees have settled here, because of the excellent standard of healthcare on offer. What's more, the government has earmarked the town – and nearby Salé, which is pretty much an extension of Rabat – for development, aiming to turn it into a vibrant tourist centre, as with many Moroccan locations. A new marina, modern residential properties, leisure facilities and shopping malls will be developed, along with five-star hotels, an artificial island covering 15 hectares and a tramway to link Salé and Rabat. It will be some time before the whole project is completed – 20 years in total – but in the meantime, it is helping to boost investment in the district.

Prices in the Rabat area tend to be on a level with Marrakesh, so are fairly high. Most investors buy along the coast, in areas such as Harhoura, Sables d'Or and Skhirate, where you can choose from apartments and bungalows for around the £120,000 (1,823,291 dirhams) mark, or sprawling villas for £250,000 (3,798,814 dirhams). Land close to the beaches varies in price from £31 to £190 (471 to 2,887 dirhams) per square metre, depending on location and proximity to the sea.

If you are looking for a traditional property, you can find some in and around the kasbah in the region of £70,000 (1,064 dirhams), while if you want to be in a more upmarket area then you can look to the Dar es Salem golf club, where purchase prices vary from £300,000 (4,562,456 dirhams) to close to £1 million (15,208,187 dirhams). In and around the American School suburb of Agdal, new apartment complexes are being constructed and here prices sit at around £30,000 to £40,000 (456,323 to 608,430 dirhams).

Souss-Massa-Draâ

Location: Central
Area: 70,880 sq km
Population: 3.1 million
Regional capital: Agadir
Property hotspots: Agadir, Ouarzazate, Aglou Plage, Mirflet, Taghazoute
Average monthly temperature/rainfall: 26.3°C/1.8 cm

This region is one of the most up-and-coming in Morocco, with low prices, stunning surroundings and massive investment from the government helping to turn it into a holiday hotspot. Stretching from the Atlantic coast, across the Atlas Mountains and on to the Algerian border, this is a varied region, which borders the desert in the south, yet has 200 miles of sandy coastline in the west. Souss-Massa is Morocco's most important national park. Lying to the south of Agadir, it stretches for 70 km and boasts cliffs, mountains, forests and farmland, and is home to a wide array of wildlife.

Agadir is southern Morocco's major tourist hotspot, set on a sweeping swathe of sand and packed with hotels, bars and restaurants. Destroyed by an earthquake in 1960 which left 17,000 of its residents dead, Agadir has long been a prosperous port and centre of trade. To the north you'll find a series of fishing villages, coves and unspoilt, undeveloped coastline in stark contrast to the area around Agadir. There's also the town of Taghazout, Morocco's finest surfing resort. Inland you'll find the lush and verdant Paradise Valley, complete with palm trees, mountain trails and waterfalls. The southern area is full of pristine, quiet beaches, along with the Spanish port of Sidi Ifni and the fine bird-watching location of Sidi

Moussa d'Aglou. Continue further south and you'll discover rocky terrain and deserts, along with a string of oases. Sitting on the edge of the Sahara and with the Anti-Atlas Mountains and their pink granite formations sweeping down the central part of the region, this is a fascinating area, and one with a colourful history.

From an investment point of view this is a hotspot, and one that should be watched carefully, especially the resort towns of Mirflet and Aglou Plage. The area has also been given a lifeline thanks to the Agadir-Marrakesh motorway, which has connected the region with the more prosperous and easily accessible north. Property for sale tends to be a blend of traditional and modern housing.

Property focus: Agadir and surrounds

One of the last major cities before you descend into the arid Saharan regions, Agadir has been developed as Morocco's premier package holiday destination, having been rebuilt after it was damaged by a serious earthquake in 1960. As a result, it lacks much traditional character, with the buildings white and uniform in nature. Nevertheless, it is located in a spectacular location, surrounded by mountains and set within a sandy white cove.

The property market here is currently hotting up, as with much of Morocco. This is a great holiday destination and will offer excellent rental returns, given that the city is geared up for beach tourism – there are modern apartments blocks, an expansive white-sand beach, bars, five-star hotels, ice cream parlours, nightclubs, casinos, excellent windsurfing, bars and supermarkets selling modern products. With cheap flights into Agadir and year-round sunshine, this resort has the potential to be massive, although it does smack of Europe rather than Africa.

The majority of properties are modern cement apartments rather than the riads and dars seen elsewhere. However, this does have its advantages, such as the fact that these are new properties with clean titles. There has been a growth in the number of villas being built, thanks to Plan Azur and the spurt in tourist numbers to the area. This is good news for investors as property prices are already starting to appreciate – one year ago you could have found a two- to three-bedroom apartment for under £40,000 (608,430 dirhams), but today you will be lucky to find much for less than £70,000 (1,064,329 dirhams).

Exclusive areas include Founty, where prices range from £150,000 to £250,000 (2,280,666 to 3,801,110 dirhams) for a luxury villa, while for something more practical, you could look to the revitalised port area, with its new marina, shops, restaurants and apartments. A newly built three-bedroom apartment here will set you back by £264,000 (4,013,972 dirhams) for direct beach access and a mooring berth.

In the Elligh area, there is a new development of apartments starting at £33,000 (501,705 dirhams) for two bedrooms with city views, garden access and proximity to the beach. Other upcoming areas lie to the north of the city and include Les Amicales and Charaf, only 15 minutes from the beach. Prices vary from between £30,000 (456,095 dirhams) and £70,000 (1,064,329 dirhams) for an apart- ment. If you're looking to buy in the centre of Agadir, expect to pay around £90,000 (1,368,265) for a modern apartment.

The suburbs

The area to the north of Agadir is government-owned land, which is only allowed to be bought by property developers and not private individuals. Also to the north of Agadir is Idi Wadden, a holiday village which has been constructed and sells one- to two-bedroom properties for £25,000 (380,073 dirhams), while in Aourir – an area known for its banana plantations and excellent beaches for surfing – you can buy a traditional property with three bedrooms for £30,000 (456,095 dirhams). In the nearby surfing resort of

Taghazoute – one of the six coastal resorts to be developed under Plan Azur – a two-bedroom property which will eventually be close to spa and golfing facilities, as well as the beach, can be yours for £111,000 (1,687,521 dirhams).

Aglou Plage

To Agadir's south, things are also changing. This area is much less developed than the north, and is attracting foreign buyers looking for a more peaceful and unspoilt location. Aglou Plage is an idyllic fishing village which is becoming increasingly popular with overseas buyers, with roughly half the population of the town being foreigners. There are many resale homes in Aglou Plage which have been bought and renovated by overseas investors, although these are obviously more costly than unrenovated properties; however, the advantage is that they hold a title. If you are looking for something traditional, there are plenty of white, sugar-cube-shaped, authentic fishermen's cottages to choose from, or increasing numbers of modern properties, thanks to the many developers buying and building here.

Aglou has been touted as an up-and-coming hotspot. There are plenty of restaurants, bars, boutiques and art galleries, and property prices are still very reasonable, for instance, the newly constructed Aglou Paradise complex of 12 luxury villas offer three-bedroom villas for £282,000 (4,252,471 dirhams), including costs.

Nearby Mirflet is also beginning to show on the investor radar. As it has long been popular with affluent French buyers, prices here are fairly high in Moroccan terms, at £160,000 (2,429,983 dirhams) for a restored villa property and £1,343 (20,396 dirhams) per square metre in the nearby Gardens of Fedela development. Nevertheless, Mirflet has been touted as the next big thing in Morocco. Less stable is the market around Sidi Ifni, where prices can vary dramatically. However, if you are buying for the lifestyle, this is a charming resort town, where prices for a costal fishermen's cottage are as little as

£10,000 to £20,000 (151,870 to 303,741 dirhams), although appreciation rates are highly variable at present.

Tadla-Azilal

Location: Central Morocco
Area: 17,125 sq km
Population: 1.45 million
Regional capital: Beni Mellal
Property hotspots: Beni Mellal
Average monthly temperature/rainfall: 26.3°C/1.8 cm

Bordering the regions of Marrakesh, Agadir to the south and Meknès to the north, the landlocked Tadla-Azilal is a largely mountainous area, sandwiched between the High and Middle Atlas Mountains. 60% of the population work in agriculture, although tourism is developing in the area, with climbing, skiing, trekking and caving all available here. It is well located with Marrakesh lying close to the west, and while this can attract passersby, there are few reasons to stay in Tadla-Azilal, due to the rugged terrain and lack of interesting conurbations. Consequently, there is little of interest for tourists and investors alike, a problem further exacerbated by the fact this is a highly inaccessible area. However, outdoor enthusiasts or those looking to set up an ecotourism business may well consider looking here.

The main city of Beni Mellal, home to 400,000 people, is a historic centre which has been protected from development by its ancient sites – the walls of the city and the Kasbah bel-Kush date back to the times of Mawlay Ismail in 1688. One of Morocco's fastest growing centres and the regional transport artery, Beni Mellal is also a market town with olives and oranges grown on the plains around it, and a large souk held on Tuesdays. Just 35 km away you'll find the Middle Atlas' largest market being held every Saturday.

Investment is limited here, most notably because many of the properties require intensive renovation and lack any services, with the majority in highly isolated locations. There are also issues of the classification of land as agricultural. Consequently, buyers will be required to cut through much red tape and complete stacks of paperwork in order to buy (see Chapter 6 for more on conveyancing).

Tangier-Tétouan

Location: North-west Morocco
Area: 11,570 sq km
Population: 2.5 million
Regional capital: Tangier
Property hotspots: Tangier, Tetouan, Chefchaouen
Average monthly temperature/rainfall: 22°C/4.15 cm

Did you know?
Myth states that Tangier was supposedly founded by Sophax, son of Greek demi-God Hercules, who named it after his mother, Tingis.

Previously a hotspot for crime and prostitution, this north-eastern region of Morocco has been a rather neglected area, although it has been cleaned up substantially in recent times as the government tries to encourage tourism into the region. Comprising Morocco's north-western tip and the city of Tangier, there are many investment hotspots here and, as well as cosmopolitan cities, there are also numerous mountain villages situated in the Rif, along with sleepy fishing villages to choose from. Tangier is also home to the elegant port of Asilah, which has been heavily influenced by the Portuguese, and Larache, the beach resort popular with Moroccan tourists. Off the northern coast of the region are the Straits of Gibraltar – with Spain essentially a stone's throw away – while to the west sits the Atlantic Ocean, with the Rif Mountains sweeping down from Tetouan into the neighbouring region of Taza-Al Hoceima-Taounate.

This area has a chequered history. During the years of protectorate it was colonised by the Spanish, with Tangier named an international zone – hence it became a magnet for crime and lowlives. Overlooked by the previous King, thanks to his dislike of the Berber Tribes who inhabited the Rif Mountains, today there has been an intense focus on developing this area. With a new and improved infrastructure, which consists of two new motorways being built, Tangier has been earmarked as a city with enormous potential, thanks largely to the two new developments that are being constructed.

Tangier is very different to the rest of Morocco, largely due to the fact that it spent many years under Spanish rule and consequently Spanish, rather than French, is the first language here. A mish mash of the elegant and squalid, Tangier was fought over for many years because of its strategically important location for trade, and nearly every inhabitant has left its indelible mark in some way or another. Tangier boasts a small medina and a number of sites including its Grand Mosque and Kasbah. Home to writers, musicians and artists of every ilk over the years – most notably the Rolling Stones and American author Paul Bowles – it was a haven for the hedonistic, and while these days may be behind it, Tangier is still regarded as a mecca for the artistic. Funding in the area has been extensive and has come not only from the Moroccan government but also the EU, which is keen to end the area's dependence on the drug trade.

Only 55 km from Tangier is Tetouan, one of Morocco's gastronomic capitals and a bustling centre that was once capital of the Spanish protectorate. The first Moroccan town you reach if you enter the country through the enclave of Ceuta, this crowded city has a modern medina – the Spanish installed street lights here during their stay – a couple of beaches and some interesting souks complete with a number of hustlers (Tetouan has a bad reputation on that front). A mix of tiled and whitewashed buildings, this town is a blend of the Hispanic and Arabic, and very much a traditional place that until recently was extremely unwelcoming to foreigners.

100

Travel to the foot of the Rif Mountains and you'll come across the town of Chefchaouen, founded by one of the descendants of the Prophet, and considered a sacred location by Muslims due to the presence of the tomb of a saint. A charming town with a small medina, souk and Jewish quarter, this has long been on the tourist backpacker route, and is well worth a look, surrounded as it is by mountains and lush countryside. Spanish influence also extends here, and is noticeable in the red tiled roofs and brightly painted houses.

Property focus: Tangier

Situated in the northern tip of the country, Tangier is an emerging hotspot. An industrial port and cosmopolitan centre, it's the driving force behind the industry and economy of northern Morocco, and the focal point for many of the infrastructure improvements which are taking place, with many new motorways being built – the Casablanca–Tangier highway opened back in 2005. Tangier is also regarded as the gateway to Spain, being only 14 km from the Spanish coast and with an underwater tunnel designed to connect Gibraltar and Tangier planned to begin construction in 2008. With flight times of less than two hours from the UK, the market is set to expand dramatically, especially with the launch at the start of 2008 of the first direct budget flight into Tangier from Madrid, with easyJet.

A real success story, up until as recently as five years ago, Tangier was a haven for drug runners and prostitutes, but today it is a thriving metropolis, thanks to EU and government investment. The current Governor, Mohammed Hassad, has been charged with transforming it into one of Morocco's most successful tourist centres, and shops, cafes and restaurants have appeared in their droves, while newly built apartment blocks now line the wide boulevards and beachfronts. There are currently two projects in place to transform the city, the first being the Tangier City Centre project, which will see £42 million invested in a tourist zone comprising hotels, cafes, restaurants, offices and residential properties. The second is the Tangier Med development, which is aimed at encouraging trade, and will see a brand new port and free trade zone established in Ksar es Sghir, 35 km outside Tangier – this will cost £625 million and provide jobs for 145,000 people.

Three years ago, land was practically being given away in an attempt to encourage development. Today, property prices are nearly on a par with Marrakesh, following the government initiatives to develop the city. A two-bedroom coastal apartment can be purchased here for £90,696 (1,370,966 dirhams), and the best option is generally to purchase in one of the many off-plan developments being constructed. Property prices on resorts such as Playa Vista start from £60,000 (906,964 dirhams), while apartments in the centre are selling from £60,000 (906,964 dirhams) for two bedrooms. Villas in the smarter areas of Marshan and restored riads in the medina start at around £150,000 (2,267,387 dirhams), with the kasbah the main centre for demand in the medina. However, properties rarely come up here as most of the riads have already been restored. Prices start from £40,000 to £90,000 (604,636 to 1,360,432) for a property in Tangier, although as demand is limited and investment levels are set to soar, this is sure to rise.

The suburbs

Areas surrounding Tangier tend to be quiet residential suburbs, such as California, where three-bedroom houses can be purchased for around £100,000 to £120,000 (1,511,339 to 1,813,607 dirhams). La Montagne is another popular location and in both areas you will find many sprawling, five-bedroom Spanish-style villas with pools that cost upwards of £320,000 (4,836,286 dirhams); land can be bought for £50 (755 dirhams) per square metre. Other areas include Cape Spartel, which is the point where the Atlantic meets the Mediterranean. Property here can be pricey, although if you settle

102

for a beachfront apartment you can buy for less than £60,000 (906,844 dirhams).

Tetouan

Tetouan is situated further down the Mediterranean coast, and is very Andalucian in appearance. Set against the backdrop of the Rif Mountains, the town is surrounded by fruit trees and olive groves, providing it with a picturesque backdrop. Its medina is Spanish in style and has been granted UNESCO World Heritage status. To purchase a property here you would be looking at under £100,000 (1,511,339 dirhams), although demand is limited and availability restricted. Foreigners tend to buy in the new developments along the coast, such as the Playa Vista, which offers two-bedroom properties from £59,900 (905,422 dirhams); Colina Smir, which has one- to three-bedroom apartments from £50,000 (755,778 dirhams); Paradise Beach and Golf Resort where two-bedroom apartments start from £73,000 (1,103,436 dirhams); and Palm Beach Resort where you can buy a two-bedroom property from £66,800 (1,009,903 dirhams).

Taza-Al Hoceima-Taounate

Location: North Morocco
Area: 24,155 sq km
Population: 1.8 million
Regional capital: Al Hoceima
Property hotspots: Taza, Al Hoceima
Average monthly temperature/rainfall: 22°C/1.9 cm

Most of the population of this rugged mountain region live in rural areas, surrounded by the Rif Mountains. Taza-Al Hoceima-Taounate borders the Mediterranean to the north, while to the south the border is marked by the gap between the Rif and Middle Atlas Mountains. Olives, figs, almonds and cereals are the main crop farmed here, while cannabis is another lucrative product which is sold to many of the foreign backpackers that tread the routes through the mountains.

A region of valleys juxtaposed with the harsh mountainous terrain and thin, poor soils of the Rif, this area is split in two by the mountains, which cut Morocco's central area off from the Mediterranean coast. For centuries, the Rif have been home to some of the country's poorest people – and the most fiercely resistant to invaders and the government alike. They have also been among the most neglected. Steps are currently being taken to reinvigorate this region and also improve its relations with the rest of Morocco, most notably with infrastructure developments. However, the main sticking point is how to deal with the reliance on cannabis production. The Rif currently produces a staggering 42% of the world's hashish, and to end production would leave the majority of the residents here without work or a livelihood.

The regional capital of Al Hoceima is strikingly distinct from the rest of this rural region. Located on the Mediterranean coast, it has been dubbed a international resort by the Moroccan tourist board and while it is not the tourism hub it may be marketed as, it is a pleasant, laid-back place that's very different from the rest of the Mediterranean resorts. Built around a small fishing port, there are white sandy beaches and wide boulevards, with a strong Spanish influence evident in the whitewashed houses.

The only other town of note in this region is Taza, also the name of one of the region's provinces. Taza is a place of great historical import, home to one of Morocco's oldest medinas, which was built in the 10th century. The capital of Morocco under the Almohad, Merenid and Alaouite rulers, surprisingly little remains of its rich history, although what does tends to be shut to westerners. The town is attractive though, and surrounded by the Djebel Tazzeka national park.

Currently, there is very little foreign interest in property in the region, although as the Mediterranean coastline has become increasingly popular, prices in Al Hoceima have begun to rise. Nevertheless, property still remains competitively priced compared with the UK. In Taza, there is no foreign demand for homes, although as accessibility into the area improves it is expected that interest in houses here will rise.

Property focus: Plan Azur resorts

Part of the ambitious 2010 plan is the development of six new resorts, all of which are set to see massive price hikes over the next few years. The flagship resort is Saïdia, although there are some still to launch, such as Port Lixus on the Atlantic coast, close to the Roman ruins in Larache.

Mediterrania Saïdia

See the Mediterranean Coast on page 86.

Port Lixus

Situated near Larache on the north Atlantic coast, this resort was launched in early 2007 and comprises two 18-hole golf courses, a new marina, a sports and leisure complex, several hotels and a number of luxurious residential buildings. Earmarked for completion in 2011, the construction will cost €1 billion and cover 4.6 million square metres. The price for a two-bedroom apartment with sea and golf course views starts at £185,000 (2,810,365 dirhams) and will be ready for 2009.

Mazagan

This resort is situated near El Jadida on the Atlantic coast and will include a world-class casino, two 18-hole golf courses, over 15 kilometres of beach and several hotels and luxury properties. Including three miles of beachfront, the resort is only one hour from

Casablanca International Airport. The project is expected to offer accommodation of 7,600 beds, including 3,700 hotel beds. Completion on one residential complex is due for 2008, and a property in the Les Palmiers de Casablanca Beach Resort will start from £48,500 (736,798 dirhams).

Mogador Essaouira

Also due to be launched in late 2007, this resort will cover 5.7 million square metres and will include two 18-hole Gary Player golf courses. The properties and hotels on offer will be extremely luxurious and will sit only three kilometres from the beach resort of Essaouira. Due for completion by 2009, prices start from around £45,000 (683,691 dirhams) for a one-bedroom apartment.

Taghazout

This $2 billion project will be situated close to Agadir on the southern Atlantic coast. Designed as a world-class tourist destination, the development will include several four- and five-star hotels, two golf courses, and several residential, leisure and retail facilities, all on three miles of sandy beach with excellent surfing to be enjoyed. Phase 1 properties are due for completion in 2008, with the first residential units, hotel, medina and golf course expected to open in early 2009.

Plage Blanche

Situated to the north of the country, close to Tangier, this project has been in question for some time, but rights to develop were recently awarded to Fadesa, the main developer of Mediterrania Saïdia.

Developers

The following developers have been given tenders for the Plan Azur Resorts:

- Saïdia: Fadesa
- Mogador: Thomas & Piron, l'Atelier, Colbert Orco and Risma
- El Haouzia: Kerzner International/SOMED/CDG/MAMDA and MCMA
- Lixus: Thomas & Piron and Orco
- Taghazout: Colony Capital and Satocan Group
- Plage Blanche: Fadesa

4
Finding a home

Once you've established where you are going to buy your new property and what you intend to buy, the next step is to go about finding your dream home.

FIXING YOUR BUDGET

This is always the most important part of planning your property purchase and, whatever type of property you intend to buy, before you begin house hunting it is essential to have established the perimeters for your budget and ideally to have factored in a contingency plan should things become more costly than you originally intended.

So, how do you establish how much to spend? It all depends on your usage and where you choose to buy. If you intend to relocate to Morocco, you may already own a property in the UK that you can sell, investing the equity in your new home overseas. Have you got any savings or a source of rental income that can go towards a purchase? Do you need to save a certain amount of money before you begin your property search and, if so, how much? Pre-empt any additional costs – such as property tax and notaries' fees – and sit down and do the sums, detailing all the costs you may incur throughout the purchasing process. Conveyancing costs vary from 5% to 12.5% of the value of the property depending on the services you require. Additional costs to be taken into account are as follows:

✓ Legal fees: generally 5.5% (this includes notary fees and registration taxes)

✓ Agent's fees: 5% to 10%

✓ Deposit: 10% to 40%

✓ Mortgage repayments

✓ Survey costs

✓ Fittings and furnishings

Before committing to a purchase, if you aren't going to be buying the property outright, then always check you will be able to raise any required cash through a mortgage or loan, and work out how much you'll be entitled to borrow. Many mortgage companies have websites that offer an online budget planner service which will give you a rough guide to how much you will be allowed to borrow. You also need to factor in the cost of the deposit. This varies depending on what you decide to buy and starts at 10% for a resale, rising to 40% for a new build, so ensure you find out exactly how much you'll be required to pay when you sign the preliminary contract to avoid any nasty shocks.

If you are buying a newly built property, figuring out how much you will be required to pay is a straightforward process – most of the costs are covered in the list above. Don't forget details such as paying a community upkeep fee. This will vary depending on the developer you choose to buy with, but is generally around £10 per square metre.

If you are looking to renovate a property then budgeting for the process does get slightly more complicated. Renovation requires a strict budget and regardless of where you buy, the rules are the same as if renovating in the UK. You shouldn't always assume that just because you are renovating in Morocco this means cheaper costs – in fact, in some areas the high demand for renovations means it can be very hard to find a good builder. Always do your research and price up potential renovation costs, making sure you get a thorough survey done prior to agreeing to buy. Generally, a renovation budget should allow for an additional 15% contingency amount should the process cost more than you accounted for – and it generally does.

Whatever your final decision may be, never throw caution to the wind, don't listen to persuasive, slick-talking agents and don't be rushed into anything. There are very few people who don't have to worry about sticking to a budget, so take care. You certainly wouldn't buy a property in the UK if you didn't have the money, so why should Morocco be any different?

Managing your budget

As we have already established, careful handling of your budget is a top priority when it comes to buying a second home. International financial experts Blevins Franks (www.blevinsfranks.com) offers some top tips to help you manage your budget wisely:

1. Before buying, always consider the maximum you can afford to pay for your property, whether you are buying in cash or raising a mortgage. If purchasing by the latter, make sure you allow for a significant rise in interest rates. If you don't and interest rates rise, you are jeopardising your ownership.
2. Don't let sweet-talking estate agents tempt you into buying more than you can afford. Buying off-plan in order to make money on completion of the build is a high-risk strategy and can lead to significant losses.
3. Always secure your mortgage in your local currency (i.e. the pound sterling in the UK). If you don't, you run the risk of suffering from a sudden fluctuation in the exchange rate. For example, if you borrow in euros at a rate of 2% and the exchange rate fluctuates, you could be faced with paying a lot more than you originally borrowed. Consequently, always employ the services of an experienced financial exchange company.
4. Always appoint an independent lawyer and, if possible, don't use the vendor's lawyer – if a problem arises, who is the lawyer advising objectively? If the developer or vendor is passing a number of clients onto a lawyer or is a 'local', then you may become the victim of poor or less than objective legal advice.
5. Never pass money for a deposit to any intermediary other than the lawyer acting for you. Even then, ask for proof that they have a segregated client account in which the funds are held, so you have some protection in the event of the lawyer running off.
6. If buying a new property, always ask the developer if they have insurance against insolvency so that if they go bust, you can claim for the lost deposit(s) and/or the right to funds to complete the project.

7. Always check the Land Registry to ensure that there are no legal charges against the land or property you are considering buying, as many builders allow a bank to have a charge against the asset pending the completion. If the builder goes bust during the build, the bank can call in the security and you may get nothing.
8. Always check that the property actually has a title. If it doesn't you will have to pay an additional 1.5% to 2.5% of the value of the property to obtain one.

RESEARCHING THE PURCHASE

There are a variety of methods and sources available to you when you're researching the purchase of your dream home, but the recommended – and most common – starting point is the internet. There is a wealth of material out there and by surfing the net you can get a better idea of the type of agent you need, the kind of property and prices you'll be looking at, as well as a cache of contacts you can arrange to meet. Never commit to an agent or property online and don't put any money forward, even if you're assured that it doesn't tie you to anything.

Search engines such as Google are a handy starting point for your web-based research. Terms such as 'Morocco property' or 'Moroccan estate agent' won't necessarily throw up hundreds of results, and information online can be limited or turn up more commonly in French than English. Nevertheless, it can be a good starting point, so keep a list or bookmark all your favourite sites so they can be easily found again.

Morocco is still a relatively up-and-coming destination, so there are few publications specifically dedicated to purchasing in Morocco. However, there are numerous property magazines and newspapers out there that are filled with useful advice and contacts for lawyers, estate agents and property finders, and they are a mine of information. For example, the weekend broadsheets and the wealth of magazines in your local newsagent are all good starting points, as are online resources such as World of Property (www.worldof property.co.uk).

For more personal advice you can attend exhibitions. This gives you the chance to meet some of the agents face-to-face and also allows you to pick up literature on developments, countries and the purchasing process. You can discuss the market and get advice about the right investment for you. Many also offer useful seminars which can help you get to grips with the state of affairs in a specific country. A list of these and all the exhibitors are available online. Go armed with a list of questions and a large bag to carry all the brochures home in, but beware the seductive spiel of some agents who will try to commit you to a sale then and there.

Exhibition contacts

- A Place in the Sun: www.aplaceinthesunlive.com
- Homes Overseas: www.homesoverseas.co.uk/Exhibitions
- International Holiday and Overseas Property Show: www.premierexhibitions.com
- www.internationalpropertyshow.com
- Overseas Property Expo: www.overseaspropertyexpo.com/
- Property Investor: www.propertyinvestor.co.uk
- The First Time Buyers Property Show: www.firstrungnow.com
- The Homebuyer Show: www.homebuyer.co.uk
- The Sunday Business Post Property Expo 2008: www.propertyexpo.ie
- Worldwide Property Show, Resale & Rental Property Show: www.dslexhibitions.ae

If you are thinking of buying in Morocco, learn about the geography and culture and get hold of some guide books such as Lonely Planet, Rough Guides and Bradt Guides. Look at the political and economic state of the country and find out what the future prognosis for the property market is. Take a look at budget flight options and any new routes that might open up or further develop the market, and where possible, take a trip out to the country and arrange to view as many properties as you can. Make sure you visit during both summer and winter as a property can take on a whole different character during the cold winter months and during peak or off peak seasons.

FINDING AN ESTATE AGENT

So, you've established a budget, done your preliminary and background research and now you want to move to the next stage – finding an estate agent to help you in your quest to secure a pad overseas.

The essential thing to remember is to always do your homework on prospective agents before getting underway with any property searches or purchasing. It is vital to do your background research when it comes to agents as different companies may offer the same property at different prices and also charge different fees. Some agents may even try to charge to show you around properties, which is an undesirable practice and one that is best avoided.

Always try to go with a company who has come recommended from friends or family. Visit the AIPP (The Association of International Property Professionals: www.aipp.org.uk) and Fopdac (The Federation of Overseas Property Developers, Agents and Consultants: www.fopdac.com) websites and check out their list of vetted agents and lawyers. There's also the International Real Estate Federation (www.fiabci.com) and the Confederation of European Real Estate Agents (www.webcei.com).

Using a Moroccan-based agent

In Morocco there are numerous estate agents, but what you need to establish is whether or not they are official or unofficial operators. It is not essential for estate agents to be registered in Morocco, so you should be careful as to who you work with. Under no circumstances should you hand over your deposit or funds to your agent – always use your notary (*notaire*), who will have an escrow account specifically for this purpose.

If you are going to use a Moroccan estate agent, always go with an official one – they will have a government-stamped licence – a *roksha* – which will certify their status. More than likely they will also be the ones with the proper offices, a website and brochure, rather than a handwritten sign!

Estate agents in Morocco are known as *agence immobiliere* or *simsaar* and they generally charge commission at a rate of 5%, although some may charge up to 10% so always ask before getting involved – some may be negotiable on this amount. Even though they are registered as official, the service will vary from one agent to another. Some may only deal with certain areas, which is more than likely, and they may or may not have links to a reliable notary. You may find you need to hand over power of attorney to them, so you need to be sure you can trust them, and the only way to be sure you can is to work with an agent who has been recommended to you. What you should also bear in mind is that the seller is king in Morocco, and they will offer the sale of their property to a number of agents, and so you should be aware that agents may be offering the same property to potential buyers at different prices. It would be preferable to secure the services of an agent who speaks English – and many do. If they don't ensure you get everything translated and get a French speaker to accompany you on your trips to the office and on viewings.

A good estate agent should be able to guide you through the conveyancing process, check whether or not a property is titled, find you a good range of properties to choose from – whether ones that are already on their books or through local contacts – and recommend a notary. If they are based in Morocco and registered, then this will be their daily job and they will know the area well and be able to offer an invaluable insight into the property market. Whatever you do, if you see an agent selling a property at a higher price than elsewhere, don't buy through them. Similarly, if an agent is pushy then walk away. In both cases they may well be trying to get a higher purchase price to ensure they get the highest amount of commission possible from the sale.

Using a UK-based agent

Morocco is an up-and-coming market and consequently there are a growing number of agents who sell property in Morocco from the UK – that said, there are nowhere near the amount you would see if you were looking to buy in France, Spain, Italy or Bulgaria. Most offer properties in developments and steer clear of the potential minefield of selling a resale property that may or may not have a title, and most concentrate on Marrakesh, Fès, Essaouira and the Plan Azur resorts.

Obviously, for those people who would prefer to work with an English-speaking agent based in the UK then this is the preferred way of doing business. However, bear in mind that these UK-based agents have only recently started selling in Morocco, and for many years before their arrival on the scene, many British and French buyers had been purchasing quite happily through Moroccan-based agents. A UK agent will generally arrange inspection visits to sites, find you a Moroccan-based notary and English-speaking lawyers and officials to guide you through the conveyancing system.

Recommendations for choosing an estate agent

◆ Try to get a recommendation – this is the best way to vet an agent.

◆ Always ask an agent if they are regulated and ask if you can see their certification.

◆ Employ someone who knows the area well and knows how the purchasing process works in the country – this could save a lot of hassle in the long run when it comes to paperwork and red tape.

◆ Make sure the agent has a good selection of property on their books – this will not only provide you with ample choice but also reveals that they are a proactive company.

◆ Whoever you choose to work with, always make sure you keep a record of your conversations and dealings with them, and keep pestering – the last thing you want is to be forgotten under a pile of other clients.

◆ The key to avoid being scammed is to do your research. If you go to an agent armed with background knowledge, this will make them realise that not only are you serious as an investor, but that they can't pull the wool over your eyes.

They will also be able to do a better job for you if they know your budget, limitations and exactly what you are looking for.

◆ Always ensure you get all documentation translated, and if the agent doesn't speak English, take a French speaker with you to ensure you are fully aware of what is being said.

Buying independently

This is always an option, and many people would prefer to do it this way than pay 2.5% commission. However, you need to be really careful and you should avoid buying a resale home which may not have a title if you decide to go it alone. If you are going to buy privately then options include simply asking locals and friends if they know anyone who is looking to sell. Whatever you do, avoid rushing into anything or appearing overly keen as this will encourage people to try to charge you above the going rate.

FACTORS TO CONSIDER WHEN CHOOSING A LOCATION

There are a number of factors that will affect your decision on where and what to buy. For a start there are budgetry issues, such as one area being cheaper than another. Then there are issues such as accessibility, your preferred location, climate and terrain and your proximity to English-speakers.

However, the first rule is to think about your personal requirements and what you want from your property, and it is essential that wherever and whatever you choose, you buy a property that fits with your intended usage. For example, if you're looking to invest, you need to assess whether the current market climate will suit buying off-plan or a plot of land. If you are purchasing a holiday home then you need to decide what you will be spending your time doing in Morocco and what your motivation is for purchasing.

If your intention is to relax on the beach, then you will be looking at the Mediterranean or Atlantic coastline. Do you want to be near mountains or in the countryside? This will obviously affect where you buy. Do you intend to let your property? If so, you will need to ensure the furnishings are appropriate and the property is close to attractions and the airport. Accessibility is another factor to take into account and if you intend to be hopping from the UK to Morocco quite regularly then you will need to be close to one of the country's international airports offering budget flights.

Morocco has a broad range of landscapes, locations and property types to choose from and so being clear on what you want from the start of your search will make the process quicker and easier, saving you time and money in the long run.

Finally, how much are you prepared to risk when purchasing? Are you happy to look at up-and-coming markets which may carry some risk but more gain in the long run – for example, the more industrialised cities of Tangier and Casablanca – or are you after a more established market such as Marrakesh or Fès?

The easiest way to narrow your search is to ask yourself some questions, such as, do you want to be near a beach? Do you want to have neighbours or would you rather live in an isolated area? Are you looking to let your property and, if so, do you want to buy within half an hour's drive of the airport, which will ultimately be more expensive? Are you buying a holiday home or purchasing as an investment? Are you going to be relocating or retiring to your property? If so, you need to consider proximity to schools and hospitals.

Insider info

Adam Cornwell, Managing Director of GEM Estates, offers some advice on choosing where to buy in the coming months.

Currently, costal resorts like Mediterrania Saïdia are hugely popular with foreign buyers because they appeal to a wide audience who want modern facilities and a nice, sweeping, sandy beach. Marrakesh will always appeal to the trendy investors who love the mix of old and new, the charm and passion of the souks, and the traditional Djemaa El Fna juxtaposed against the chic restaurants and Nikki Beach of the Palmeraie, Marrakesh's own Beverly Hills. Those who take the time to study the figures (hotel occupancy, potential rental returns, enormous increases in tourist arrivals, etc.) will realise that it is no coincidence that GEM Estates has two products with nine- to ten-year rental guarantees that are in Marrakesh. Finally new spots such as Mirleft, the quiet fishing village and chill-out resort perched between the desert and the sea just south of Agadir, are also beginning to look interesting.

Issues to consider

Where
◆ Do you want to live in the city or countryside?

◆ Do you want to be inland, near the coast, or close to the mountains?

◆ Is your wish to live in an isolated community or do you want to have neighbours?

◆ Is good weather important to you or are you happy to endure cooler winters?

◆ How important is accessibility and do you need to be near airports, schools, shops, etc?

◆ Do you want to be close to English speakers or are you happy to immerse yourself into the local community?

Why
◆ Why do you want to buy your property? Are you going to be using it for weekend breaks/months away/holidays? Are you looking to relocate, or is it a pure investment?

◆ Do you want to make money from your home?

◆ Do you eventually intend to retire here?

◆ If you intend to sell the property later, are other properties in the area selling well?

Travel
◆ Are the cost of flights expensive and do you need to transfer or can you fly direct? If you intend to rent the property, make sure you buy close to an airport that offers budget flights.

◆ Are you happy to go to the same place every year?

◆ Is accessibility an issue? If you intend to retire here, will it remain just as easy to access when you are older?

◆ Do you need a car in order to travel about or is there public transport available?

Amenities
◆ Do you want shops, restaurants, etc. on your doorstep or are you happy to travel to reach them?

◆ Do you have hobbies/sports you want to pursue?

◆ What entertainment could you enjoy in the area?

◆ Do you need to be close to the office/school?

Health
◆ Does anyone in the family have long-term health concerns – e.g. diabetes or heart problems – that will need to be regularly monitored?

◆ How good is your local doctor or hospital?

◆ How near will you be to the doctor/dentist/hospital?

Practicalities
◆ Is it important to be able to speak the language? If so, are you prepared to learn?

◆ Do you want to take your pet(s) and children?

◆ Do you know your neighbours?

◆ Do you feel able to get to grips with the Islamic lifestyle, which is very different?

◆ Are there expats in the area? If not, are you prepared to integrate yourself into local life?

Type
◆ Who will be staying/living in the property? Will it just be yourself and your partner, or are you likely to have family and friends round? If so, you will need to ensure there is space/spare rooms.

◆ Will you need to modernise the property? If so, have you budgeted for renovation costs, which can be very high in Morocco?

◆ Do you want a property with character or something new and pristine with all mod cons?

TRYING BEFORE YOU BUY

You wouldn't buy a car without taking it for a test drive, having already visited numerous garages, and nor should you commit to buying a property without having first visited the area and looked at a number of different properties. The biggest mistake you can make is to commit to buying a property without travelling out to the country and checking the area – and the property – first. Even if you have employed the services of a house search agency, get them to narrow the options down and take a week out to go and view them all.

Getting to know Morocco before you buy is essential – and also the most fun bit of the purchasing process. Try to travel extensively around the country before making any firm decisions – remember, Morocco is extremely diverse and there are a number of different locations to choose from. Buy a map and guidebook and make notes, take photos and check out exactly what facilities would be available to you if you bought there.

The best way to see everything is to take as much time as possible AND to rent a property in the area, hire a car and spend time living there as you would if you had bought a home there. This is the closest you can get to experiencing what life would be like, and also gives you a chance to meet and talk with the locals, and try to discover what the area is really like.

Inspection trips are another way to spend time experiencing a country, and doing this can help you to make an informed purchase. However, there are disadvantages and inspection trips have had bad press in the past, thanks to the use of aggressive sales techniques and the bullying of clients. If you do choose to go on a viewing trip then don't let yourself be pressured into anything.

On the positive side, there are many advantages to viewing trips. For one thing you will be provided with a portfolio of properties to visit that meet your specifications, you'll get to know your estate agents, you'll be provided with subsidised flights and accommodation and you will have the opportunity to get to know the country and the purchasing process. These can be genuinely helpful trips, but do not treat them as free holidays and ensure you know exactly what costs you are likely to incur.

5
Finance and taxation

FINANCING YOUR PURCHASE

Obviously, the first hurdle to overcome when looking to buy a property in Morocco is the financing of your purchase. Since becoming a property hotspot, and thanks to the government's desire to encourage investment, there are several large banks in Morocco that are prepared to lend to non-resident property buyers. However, there are also other methods to consider for raising money to purchase your dream home.

Mortgages

There are no UK banks in Morocco and so in order to raise a mortgage from within the country, you have to go through one of the large Moroccan banks such as Credit Du Maroc or BMCE. UK banks currently won't offer you a mortgage against a property in Morocco and so if you decide to raise your finance in the UK, it will have to be taken out against a UK property (see page 124 on Raising finance in the UK).

Financing your purchase through a Moroccan mortgage is not the cheapest way to buy simply because the interest rate is so high at 7% to 8%. It is estimated that this will reduce in time, as applying for a mortgage becomes a more regular occurrence and the market matures. At present, the Moroccan people are generally sceptical about borrowing, so the market is primarily driven by outside borrowers.

Current interest rates sit at about 7% for a variable rate mortgage and the maximum loan-to-value is 70%, meaning you can only secure the value of 70% of the price of your property. The maximum age a borrower can be at the end of the mortgage term is 65 and mortgages are only arranged in the local currency of dirhams – however, the dirham is quite heavily pegged to the euro, limiting serious fluctuations. Another positive is the current situation in terms of the tourist market. While interest rates on mortgage repayments may be high, calculate how much income you may be able to secure from your property – two to three years of returns at 15% to 20% may make it worth getting a mortgage, offsetting the potentially high interest rates.

At present, only Capital and Interest (Repayment) mortgages are available and it is common to have to deposit five months' interest in a bank account in order to secure your mortgage. Rates are revised annually or can be fixed for as long as five years. When it comes to calculating your eligibility for a mortgage, most banks will normally lend you up to 35% to 40% of your net annual salary.

Mortgage applications must be arranged on a full-status basis, meaning applicants must submit full proof of their earned income in the form of an employment contract, your last six months of bank statements, your last three wage slips and tax returns for the last two years. If you are self-employed you must provide company registration details and a certificate of incorporation, your last two years of tax returns and audited accounts, and your last six months of bank statements.

It is common for mortgagees to open a euro account with a Moroccan bank and transfer sterling or euros into this account. The euros are then converted into dirhams to meet monthly mortgage repayments. However, potential buyers must consider the fluctuating currency risk when applying for a mortgage – after all, if the dirham fluctuates massively against the pound or sterling then this could result in your having to pay more for your mortgage than originally anticipated.

Documents required for non-residents looking to secure a mortgage

Employed

◆ P60

◆ Pay slips for three months

◆ Employer's reference

◆ Bank statements for six months

Self-employed

◆ Self-assessment tax return

◆ Accountant's reference

◆ Bank statements for six months

For both

◆ Passport

◆ Copy of purchase contract

◆ Copy of credit file

Insider info

Matthew Weston is Manager of Overseas Mortgages at financial advice group Blevins Franks (www.blevinsfranksinternational.com). He takes a look at the pros and cons of taking out a mortgage through a Moroccan bank.

The number of Moroccan banks offering mortgages to non-resident investors is steadily rising. As a former French protectorate, French banks have a strong presence in Morocco, with BNP Paribas, Crédit Foncier and Société Générale proudly flying their colours in all Moroccan towns and cities. Local Moroccan-owned banks are less adapted to lending to non-residents and you may find that they offer a more limited choice of mortgage products.

French banks in Morocco have strict lending criteria using a debt-to-income calculation to gauge how much they can lend. This is based on the percentage of gross salary spent on servicing total debt a month, and is usually set between 35% and 40%. Credit searches are commonplace. Banks are normally keen to meet the clients in person at their office.

The maximum loan-to-value (LTV) mortgage is 70% with a maximum mortgage term of 25 years, although it is more likely that a Moroccan bank will agree to a maximum LTV of 60% and the maximum term available will be around 15 years. Most mortgages are available on a Capital and Interest (Repayment) basis but some banks will offer Interest Only options for short terms of up to two years.

It is important to point out that all applications are considered on a case-by-case basis and there's no self-certification or fast-tracking of applications. Interest rates are linked to the Moroccan Taux*, which is reviewed bi-annually by the government starting on 1 January each year. The government gives banks a cap and collared rate from which to work with, and this currently stands at between 5% and 8%. Interest rates offered to foreign investors tend to be at the higher end of this scale.

*The Moroccan Taux is similar to a national base rate, setting itself out as a basis to price loans to borrowers. What is unique about the Taux is that it has a bottom and top range of rates that banks can work from.

Raising finance in the UK

In the UK, banks will only allow you to draw a mortgage against your UK property in order to finance your purchase in Morocco, and will not currently offer a specific mortgage against a Moroccan property. This means your options include remortgaging your UK home or securing a mortgage on a UK home and then using the money to help fund your purchase in Morocco.

Alternative methods for raising finance include securing a short-term loan. This is particularly popular if you know you have a lump sum of cash coming to you – such as a pension – and need a stop-gap to help pay a deposit or other purchasing-related fees. There are also facilities such as an overdraft extension or the use of a credit card, but again, while the use of these is personal preference, make sure you don't lumber yourself with more debt than you can repay as this will simply make owning a home abroad a burden rather than a pleasure.

Currency conversion

When looking to take out a mortgage in dirhams you need to be aware of the potential for currency fluctuations, which can lead to you paying an extra 10% to 20% on your mortgage – something you want to avoid at all costs. The best way to negotiate and successfully navigate currency exchange is to search for the best exchange rate deal. There are numerous specialist currency exchange companies out there who will often beat the rates offered by the high-street banks. You can choose from a risk-free option (to buy all of your currency in one go and fix the cost of exchange) or a high-risk strategy (to buy dirhams each time you need to send them to the developer/seller). There are also a number of forward-buying contracts, where you fix your foreign exchange rate for a specified amount today and elect a date in the future to pick up and pay for your currency. A deposit payment of between 3% and 10% is generally required on agreement of the contract.

There are also a number of sophisticated currency swap arrangements that individuals can enter into, but these are probably not going to be suitable for most and do not always provide complete protection.

Useful contacts

www.fidentiagroup.com
www.currencies.co.uk
www.globexfx.com
www.travelex.co.uk
www.currenciesdirect.com
www.hifx.co.uk

Insider Info

Denise Blackburn of MoneyCorp (www.moneycorp.com) explains the best way to go about organising your currency exchange.

One of the most cost-effective ways of sending your money to Morocco to buy a property is to use a foreign exchange specialist. A specialist will offer you guidance on the currency markets and will help you secure the best exchange rate for your transfer, thus saving you money. Not only this, but they should also transfer your money to Morocco much quicker than your bank.

A foreign exchange company will allow you to purchase your cash on a spot or a forward contract. A spot contract is very much like it sounds – it allows you to buy your euros immediately (and up to five days ahead). So, if you need to purchase and send your euros quickly, then a spot contract should be ideal.

A forward contract (buying forward) enables you to 'fix' an exchange rate now and for up to two years in advance. This means that you are guaranteed the rate, even if you don't require your euros for up to two years. A forward contract is ideal if you need to make stage payments on your property because it allows you to fix the cost of those payments. By fixing the exchange rate, you can protect yourself against negative rate fluctuations and you can budget effectively for the cost of your Moroccan property. To book a forward contract you will need to put down a 10% deposit and then, when the settlement date arrives, you will need to transfer the balance of the sterling. Your foreign exchange specialist will then pay your money into your account in Morocco.

After you have bought your property, if you need to arrange monthly transfers to Morocco, a foreign exchange specialist will be able to help you set up regular payments by direct debit at a fraction of the cost charged by your UK bank.

Finally, one last thing to watch out for is receiving bank fees. You may find that some Moroccan banks will charge you upon receipt of your euros, but don't worry – any reputable foreign exchange specialist should offer to pay these charges for you!

OPENING A BANK ACCOUNT

It's a relatively straightforward process to open a bank account in Morocco, and they operate in a similar way to European banks. If you intend to buy a property in Morocco then you need to open a bank account. All banks offer credit cards, telephone and online banking, and ATM access. However, there are not ATMs everywhere in Morocco and your average street vendor or taxi driver will only accept cash, while outside of major towns and cities few – if any – people will accept a credit card. As such, it is sensible to keep a supply of dirhams on you at all times.

Morocco's central bank is the Bank Al-Maghrib (www.bkam.ma) and it regulates banking operations throughout the country, with branches in all of the main cities. The following is a list of the Morocco's main banks:

◆ BMCE: www.bmcebank.ma
◆ La Banque Centrale Populaire: www.gbp.ma

- Attijariwafe Bank: www.attijariwafabank.com

- BMCI: www.bmcinet.com

- Bank Al-Maghrib: www.bkam.ma

When deciding who to bank with, be aware that most offer the same services, such as convertible bank accounts (see below), telephone banking, credit cards, etc. The major issues to consider are: does anyone in the bank speak English, where is your nearest/most accessible bank and do you need a bank with a UK-based branch? This would limit the charges incurred for transferring money to your Moroccan account.

Bank accounts

Convertible Bank Accounts

Every foreigner is automatically given a convertible account as the dirham is a restricted currency – i.e. it cannot be taken out of the country, nor can it be obtained outside of Morocco. Therefore, you can open an account into which you can pay the euro and pound sterling, and these are automatically transferred into the dirham, which is handy when it comes to transferring money to cover deposits or mortgage payments. It also means that you can repatriate currency without having to go through the Bureau de Change. However, be aware that you cannot pay the dirham into this bank account – for that you will need a local or non-convertible account.

The convertible account will provide you with a cheque book (cheques are written in French and are generally not used in the country) and a debit card (banks do not issue specific Moroccan credit cards but do accept foreign credit cards). The account must be kept active otherwise the bank will close it after one year. This account allows you to freely transfer money overseas and, in most cases, there is no minimum amount required to open one. However, this account will not pay you any interest.

127

Regular dirham account

In order to open this, many people – and banks – will tell you that you need to be a legal resident with a residency card; however, some banks will allow you to open a dirham account without a residency permit. Debit cards can be requested and issued for a regular dirham account. This account only receives dirhams, and generally speaking you won't need one unless you are actually working in Morocco and being paid in dirhams, or you have some specific dirham-related income. Be aware that this account will require you to transfer funds through the Bureau de Change in order to transfer them back home.

Banking hours

Banking hours are extremely restricted in Morocco and every bank keeps slightly different schedules, so always check what these are before choosing a bank. From July to August, the hours change again. Here are some examples of typical bank opening times:

Attijariwafa Banque, Marrakesh:

September to June

Monday to Friday: 8.15 am–11.30 am and 2.15 pm–5.00 pm

July to August

Monday to Friday: 8.15 am–3.00 pm only

MOROCCAN TAXES

The Moroccan tax system is modelled after the French system and has quite a few complexities. The whole question of taxes is something of a murky issue in Morocco, and nobody ever seems to know how much is paid or even who does actually pay tax. That said, don't take any risks as things are getting more strict and you don't want to find yourself landed with a huge tax bill five or six years down the line. For this reason it is best to obtain expert tax advice before making an investment.

Resident or non-resident?

Payment of taxes in Morocco is dependant on your status as a tax resident. You are regarded as a resident for tax purposes in Morocco if a) your main source of income is generated there, or b) you spend 183 days of the year in the country. If you have income generated in the UK, you will still be liable to pay some taxes there, but there's a dual taxation treaty in place to avoid you paying tax twice. Incidentally, just because you have a residency permit doesn't mean you automatically become a resident for tax purposes.

You will be considered a non-resident if you simply own a holiday home in Morocco and spend most of the year in the UK, earning your income there. Rental income generated must be declared to both tax offices but it will probably be payable in Morocco.

Double taxation treaty

There is a double tax treaty between the UK and Morocco that ensures investors do not have to pay taxes in both countries and that if you earn any income in Morocco which is taxed there, you won't have to pay twice – i.e. again in the UK. Any income made from your Moroccan property will have to be declared both in Morocco and in the UK, and when calculating your UK tax liability, the Inland Revenue will deduct the taxes you have already paid in Morocco.

Taxes payable

There are three main forms of tax that are payable in Morocco. These are:

Income tax (Impôt Général sur le Revenu (IGR))

The general Income Tax (IGR) was introduced in 1989, and was replaced by the Income Tax (IR) on 1 January 2006. It's levied at a progressive rate from 0% to 42%. Whether or not you pay this in

Morocco depends on your status as a resident or non-resident. If you are employed in Morocco then your income tax will be taken from your monthly pay, while if you are self-employed and earn income in Morocco, you will need to file a tax return on 1 May every year, regardless of whether you are a resident or not. Corporation tax is levied at a flat 30%, although foreign currency brought into the country is exempt from tax for the first five years. There are no income taxes to be paid for the first three years of owning a newly built property, although only the first owner can benefit from this exoneration.

Income tax is charged at a progressive rate as follows:

Annual income/Rent in DH	Rate
Up to 24,000	0%
24,001–30,000	15%
30,001–45,000	25%
45,001–60,000	35%
60,001–120,000	40%
More than 120,001	42%

When calculating the net rental incomes, the gross rental income is reduced by 40%.

Other sources of income

Life insurance: a 10% rebate of the tax contributions paid for life insurance is offered, but the rebate cannot exceed 900 dirhams per annum.

Foreign pensions: Moroccan residents who receive a pension from overseas can benefit from an 80% reduction of income tax.

Taxes on property purchase

Registration fees or Stamp Duty (Droit d'Enregistrement)

This is levied on the transfer of a property between the buyer and the seller; it can also be levied on the transfer of shares.

Fees vary depending on the type of property you buy and its intended usage. Generally, it ranges from 1% up to 10%, with the average being 2.5%. If you intend to start a business such as a hotel or B&B then you will pay a higher rate.

Notarial tax (Taxe Notariale)

If you are using a notary during your transaction – and it is recommended that you do – 0.5% to 1% of the value of the property must be paid to your notary. This covers all the work done to secure the conveyancing and is payable on the signing of the final contract.

Registration (Droits de la Conservation Foncière)

This is equivalent to the registration in the Land Registry. The applicable rate is 1% plus 150 dirhams for the certificate of property. However, as a penalty, it could be increased up to 2% if the registration is delayed for more than 18 months.

VAT (TVA)

The normal rate is 20%, introduced in 2007. It is reduced to 14% for renovations, repairs or building works. The VAT is included in the purchase price.

Council or local taxes (Taxe Urbaine and Taxe d'Édilité)

These two taxes are the equivalent of council tax in the UK and are used to cover the upkeep of your local surroundings, the maintenance of roads, the cleaning of streets, the removal of garbage, street lighting, etc. However, these taxes are only applicable to people who live in the Urban Commune and are provided with these services, if you live in a rural area you are exempt. You are also exempt if you use your property to pursue a business activity or if you are the first owner of a newly constructed property, for example an off-plan or newly built home.

Urban tax (Real estate tax (Taxe Urbaine))

This tax applies to both residential homes and buildings, although they are taxed at different levels depending on their usage. If you are making money from your property or using it for professional purposes, then your Taxe Urbaine (TU) is charged at a fixed rate of 13.5% of your annual rental income. However, a residential property is charged at a sliding scale which is calculated based on the property's annual rental value, determined by the Census Committee. This annual rental value increases by 2% every five years.

Urban tax brackets

Rental Value	Tax
Less than 3,000 dh	0%
3,001–6,000 dh	10%
6,001–12,000 dh	16%
12,001–24,000 dh	20%
24,001–36,000 dh	24%
36,001–60,000 dh	28%
More than 6,000 dh	30%

You get a 75% tax allowance if the property is your main place of residence, and if you make no income from it. There is a fixed rate of 3% for plots of land, buildings, layouts, materials and equipment.

Council or local tax (Taxe d'Édilité)

This applies to buildings built or being built and to plots of land allocated to any kind of business which lie within the Urban Commune. The taxation rate for Taxe d'Édilité is:

♦ 10% of the rental value for properties located within the areas of the urban administrative district and delimited zones.

♦ 6% of the rental value for properties located in the outlying areas of the urban administrative district.

Capital gains tax (Taxe sur le profit immobilier)

Capital gains are levied on any financial gains made on land or property when sold. You are exempted from paying capital gains tax if the property has been your main place of residence for eight years and if the capital gain realised by the owner for the year is under 60,000 dirhams. Capital gains tax is levied at a rate of 20% on all profits made from any sale over and above the value of 60,000 dirhams.

Corporation tax (IS Taxe (Impôt sur les Sociétés))

This is charged at a flat rate of 30%. However, the Tangier area benefits from a reduced rate of 17.5%.

Foreign investors who are exporting products or services to Morocco benefit from a total exoneration of the payment of corporation tax for the first five years of starting their business. After this period they benefit from a reduction of 50%.

All expenses incurred for the purpose of the business are normally deductible, including salaries and wages, depreciation, rent and representation expenses.

Trading licence (The Patente)

The Patente is the equivalent to a trading licence and has to be paid as a tax. It applies to any person who is carrying out a professional activity, an industry or business in Morocco, and there is no distinction between Moroccan and foreign citizens. The Patente is a tax paid in proportion to the current normal gross rental value of the premises, sites and facilities. You are exonerated from paying the Patente for the first five years of your business starting up, unless you are an estate agent, bank, or credit or insurance company.

Wealth tax and inheritance tax

Neither of these taxes are levied in Morocco. However, even though there is no inheritance tax to pay, purchasers may be liable to pay inheritance tax in the UK and so you are advised to contact the Inland Revenue in order to find out where you stand.

6
The buying process

Given that Morocco has been a popular destination with French buyers for many years, the conveyancing process follows the French model quite closely, and the system has been streamlined in order to make it easier for foreigners to invest in the country. The Moroccan legal system is Latin-based (i.e. a legal system that employs Latin-based terminology as in the UK), and the main problem you will come up against is the lack of a title for certain properties – for example, old riads.

While the legal process may be straightforward, given the problems with title and the fact that there may be hundreds of family members to secure approval from, you may find it easier to go with a newly built or off-plan property, which is recognised by the municipality and has a new title. The notary plays an important role in buying a property in Morocco, so ensure you find a reliable one, and while legally you don't need a lawyer to be involved in the purchase, it is recommended you use one – in many cases agents recommend you employ a local expert as well as an English lawyer.

DIFFERENCES BETWEEN THE BUYING PROCESS IN MOROCCO AND THE UK

On first glance, the two buying processes may look very similar, although there are noticeable differences between the two legal systems which means you should always get the best impartial advice possible. The main difference is that in the UK there is no need to sign a preliminary or reservation contract, plus the deposit payment in the UK is much smaller than in Morocco, where it ranges from 10% for a resale home to 40% for an off-plan property. The following table shows the main differences between buying in the UK and in Morocco.

	UK	Morocco
Stage one	Prior to the Exchange of Contracts, the draft contract is received and negotiated, enquiries are made about the property and the formal mortgage offer is received.	Once you have found a property, you enter a verbal offer, and if this is agreed you will then move on to signing a preliminary contract, which is legally binding. At this stage you will also be required to pay a deposit of between 10% and 40%.
Stage two	Exchange of Contracts: The contract is signed and you hand over a 10% deposit. Final accounts are prepared and the mortgage deed requested for you to sign.	Your notary will then obtain the title deeds. Depending on what type of property you are buying, this could be quick and easy or a complicated procedure. It will be easy with a new-build home, but it can take up to a year with an old riad, as you will have to pay for new title deeds and track down the family members to secure their approval for the sale.
Stage three	Completion: You obtain the keys to your new home and receive the title deeds. Stamp duty is paid and the transfer is arranged at the Land Registry so the house is now registered in your name.	Prior to completion, you will receive a draft version of the final contract, which you must read, sign and return to the notary once you're happy with it. The signing of the final contract must take place in the presence of the notary, although if you cannot be present, you can sign a power of attorney which will allow someone else to sign it for you. Once the final contract is signed, the remaining balance of payments and fees are due.

SURVEYS AND INSPECTIONS

There is no formal property survey system in place in Morocco, and it is not a required part of the conveyancing process. However, if you are going to be buying an old or resale property, especially with the intention to renovate, then it is recommend that you employ the services of a qualified surveyor to examine the building.

Your notary should complete a background check on the property, as well as the title deeds, to ensure there are no outstanding debts attached to the property that would be transferred with the sale. You could arrange for a visual survey too, as well as for a structural engineer to view the property. The type of report you decide to get will differ from a UK survey and is generally not as thorough, and you may have to get it translated. Bear in mind that you may need to get a survey done in order to secure a mortgage. Structural surveys typically take 7 to 10 days, and the time and cost varies from place to place.

The following is a list of things to ensure the surveyor looks out for:

◆ That the title corresponds to the property's size and number of rooms.

◆ Whether the plot boundaries are correct and accurate – not just a vague point of the finger and 'they stretch from that tree to that rock'.

◆ That the walls and roof have no obvious signs of disrepair, cracks or structural instability.

◆ That the property is not suffering from damp, salt erosion or dry rot.

◆ Which fittings and furnishings come with the house and garden and which don't.

◆ That the doors and windows fit and lock properly.

◆ Whether you are connected to utilities. If not, check whether you can be connected.

137

- The location of plug sockets and telephone points, and whether there are enough. Are there any at all or do these need to be fitted?

- Is there fully functioning heating and air conditioning or is this something you will have to add?

- Is the bathroom in good condition? Are the tiles damaged? Is the bathroom ventilated? Do you have a proper toilet or will this need to be fitted?

- Whether the drainage system functions properly.

- If there any strange smells in the house.

- Are there signs of insect infestation in the woodwork.

THE BUYING PROCEDURE: THE BASIC STEPS TO BUYING A PROPERTY

Once you have decided where to buy and found your perfect home (see Chapter 3 on locations and Chapter 4 on finding a home), then it's time to proceed with the conveyancing process and buy the property.

Stage one: Restrictions on foreign buyers

There are no restrictions on foreigners buying property in Morocco, and they are treated in the same way as residents of Morocco – in fact, you can buy as many homes as you want. However, restrictions do apply on the purchase of land, but these can be circumnavigated. See page 145 on buying land for more details.

Stage two: Initial steps to take

As well as choosing an estate agent (see Chapter 4), you also need to find a lawyer and/or a notary to work with.

Finding a notary

Unlike in the UK, where we use a lawyer, the notary (notaire) is the main figure to undertake conveyancing, and he is best placed to guide you through the processes. Under no circumstances should you choose a UK lawyer over a notary as your notary will have all the local knowledge and awareness of how the system works – it is always safest to use both.

The notary is a public officer whose main role is to make sure that all legal processes have been undertaken correctly in order to compete the sale of a property, and that all fees and taxes are paid, with the title checked. It is not difficult to find a notary in Morocco, but try to find one you feel comfortable working with and who ideally speaks English. Many estate agents can recommend a notary but if you can secure a recommendation from an impartial party then all the better. Note that the role of the notary is to make sure that the conveyancing formalities follow the legislation in place in Morocco and, unlike a solicitor in the UK, he is not paid to give purchasers impartial advice.

Finding a lawyer

The benefit of employing a lawyer is that they can offer you impartial advice on contracts and titles, unlike the notary, who is essentially a guide though the process. It is always advisable to employ an English-speaking lawyer, as not all Moroccan notaries will speak English, and to always choose a lawyer with experience of Moroccan legislation. If you go with a UK-based lawyer, make sure they have contacts or an associate in the country.

The best way to go about finding a lawyer is to contact the London-based embassy for Morocco and ask them for a list of recommended lawyers. Another simple method of hunting down a reliable professional is to secure a personal recommendation, either from family or friends or by posting a notice on an expat forum.

Stage three: Making a verbal commitment

If you have found a property that you would like to purchase, the next step is to put in a verbal offer and agree on the price. You can either put this offer forward yourself or via your estate agent, and negotiations on the price can proceed from there. You have to be careful when negotiating, as the seller may try to test your enthusiasm for the property by asking you to pay more than the original asking price! The key to a successful negotiation is to avoid appearing too keen – if you do this you may well be able to knock between 5% and 10% off the original asking price. Remember, Morocco is a buyers' market and there are still plenty of property options, so don't be forced into purchasing through threats of losing the property.

Stage four: Ownership

Once you have come to an agreement over the property price, your notary can begin drawing up the paperwork, but one key question to ask yourself is, who should own the property? This question is important when buying overseas and can have many financial implications further down the line, particularly with regard to taxes. It is a difficult question to answer here as it depends on personal circumstances and the property in question, so the best idea is to ask your lawyer for an unbiased opinion. There are many ownership options, and these are as follows.

- In your own name.
- In your name and in the name of your co-purchaser(s).
- Totally or partly in your children's names or in the name of somebody whom you would like to inherit the property from you. However, in Morocco there is no inheritance tax so this may not be a consideration.
- In the name of a limited company, whether English, Moroccan or off-shore.

♦ Via your SIPP/SSAS (Self-Invested Personal Pension/Small Self Administered Scheme) pension fund.

♦ Via an investment fund (e.g. REIT – Real Estate Investment Trust).

♦ Via an investment club.

♦ Via a trust.

To find out more, see page 149 on buying through a company.

Stage five: The Reservation Contract (Contrat de Reservation)

A Reservation Contract (Contrat de Reservation) is a short contract which allows the property to be taken off the market while the Preliminary Contract (Compromis de Vente) is drawn up. A small amount of money (typically £2,000) is paid in order to secure the reservation of the property, and your notary or lawyer can then get to work checking the title and the property background before drawing up the Preliminary Contract. The Reservation Contract will only take the property off the market for around two to four weeks and during this period you can pull out of the sale.

You should be aware that some agents will try to get you to sign a fully binding Preliminary Contract right at the start of the purchasing process. This is not really a preliminary agreement at all, but a legally binding commitment to buy the property, so always avoid working with an agent who tries to commit you to the sale right from the outset.

Stage six: The Preliminary Contract (Compromis de Vente)

Once you and the seller have come to an agreement on the sale price, the terms and conditions of the sale are discussed with the notary, who then prepares the Preliminary Contract. This contract is just as important as the final document which transfers the title and

141

completes the sale, as it will contain all the clauses, terms and conditions which govern the sale.

The main terms contained in the Compromis are as follows:

- Personal details of the seller.
- Personal details of the buyer.
- Mention of the title deed.
- Mention of planning permission.
- Object of the agreement, i.e. the property.
- Completion date.
- Sale price.
- Receipt of the deposit paid.
- Expenses and taxes to be met by the buyer.
- Condition precedents, i.e. the conditions by which you agree to the sale. For example, if your purchase depends on obtaining a mortgage in Morocco or in the UK, this should be added as a clause.
- Penalties if one of the parties withdraws from the transaction.

It then usually takes one to three months (or longer, depending on the individual circumstances) for the notary to prepare all the necessary paperwork before getting the parties together to sign the Title Deed (Acte de Vente). During this time, the notary will ask the Conservation Foncière (Land Registry) whether the property is titled (see page 143 for details on Titles) and whether there are any existing loans or other charges attributed to the property.

Be aware that this is a legally binding contract and once you have signed it, you are committed to the sale, so only sign if you are 100% happy with the terms listed in the Compromis. At this stage you are required to pay a deposit which varies from 10% for a resale or renovation property to 40% for an off-plan development property.

Beware!
A problem that you may be faced with in Morocco is that sometimes the property you are ready to purchase is occupied by a tenant or tenants, and it could happen that the house is still occupied after the sale is completed. The best advice is to pay the remaining balance for the price of the property only when the house is empty and you've inspected it. This may be a problem because the seller often needs your money to pay for their new house, preferring that the buyer doesn't move into the property until they have paid all outstanding amounts. You could ask your notary to add into the Preliminary Contract the condition that you can withhold paying the full amount for the sale of the property, until the seller has proved that the property is vacant from any occupier.

Stage seven: Title deeds

You cannot complete the purchase of your property without either a requisite title or a real deed and one of the major problems faced by foreign buyers in Morocco is the absence of title deeds. Obviously, if you are buying off-plan or a new-build you will have title deeds – although always double check this and the planning permission to ensure the development is legal – whereas a traditional, crumbling riad in the medina is unlikely to have the relevant deed. The situation with land is often similar.

Buildings that are not recorded in the land registry with all the necessary documentation and title deeds are governed by the traditional rules of Muslim law. Do not under any circumstances purchase a property or land in Morocco without obtaining the title deeds, because you can never be sure that the property or land belongs to you. Untitled properties in Morocco are known as *Melkia*. Before the existence of the notary, no title system existed. Instead, you would have been given a scroll written by an *Adoul*, an official scribe, documenting the ownership, and these would sometimes go back several hundred years – they are all obviously written in Arabic.

Most new properties – and renovated ones situated within the urban perimeter – will now have title deeds, in contrast with the unrenovated ones, and if it is a modern property you will simply have to pay 1% to have the title deeds transferred into your name. However, if the property does not have a title, then the potential buyer will have to pay around 2.5% to secure 'real deeds'. You can secure the sale with a requisite title, although you should secure real deeds wherever possible. To do this, you need to be prepared to wait for up to a year as it will mean the Land Registry Office has to send out a surveyor to measure the plot and property, with a notice of sale being listed in the Land Registry and commune for four months to allow any locals or potential owners to contest the sale.

In the past, there have been cases of falsification, so it is very important that when buying you go through a notary, who is the only person who can carry out the title searches and obtain certain legal documents to make the transaction possible.

The notary will track down all the named owners of the property. Each family member then needs to consent to the sale going ahead. The advantage of this is that banks are willing to give a loan if the title process has begun and been paid for, and it is likely that a house with a title will bring a higher price in the future.

Stage eight: The Final Contract (Acte de Vente)

The purchase is only completed when the final deed of sale is signed and legal ownership is transferred to the buyer. It is at this point that the balance of the purchase price, plus any extras are due, such as the notary's fees, taxes and duties. These monies will be paid directly into the holding account of the notary, and wherever possible it is a good idea to attend the notary's office in person for the final signing and witnessing of the deed of sale. However, if this is not possible you can invoke a power of attorney and have a representative take your place.

Once the document has been signed and stamped by the notary, the deeds of the property are then recorded at the Land Registry. The Land Registry's stamp is put on the deed of sale and the notary gives a certified copy of the deed to you around two months after completion of the sale. Until you receive this copy, the notary will give you a certificate of ownership which proves that you are the owner of the property. You can use this document to connect your house to electricity and water, and even to sell your property. The whole process from the initial reservation up to the final signing takes around 12 to 16 weeks, provided there are no hold-ups with the title deeds.

Typical costs

♦ Legal fees stand at around 5.5% of the purchase price and are paid by the buyer.

♦ Estate agent's fees are charged at a rate of 5% to 10%.

♦ Taxes on completion come to around 5% of the purchase price. This includes Stamp Duty, 2.5% Registration Tax and 0.5% Notary Tax.

♦ Capital gains tax is 20% on profits over €60,000. After five years, capital gains tax reduces to 10% and after eight years it reduces to zero.

♦ If you are planning on renting out your property once it's completed there is no rental tax for five years.

♦ There is no inheritance tax to pay in Morocco if you leave your property to a family member. You may be liable to pay inheritance tax back in the UK though – always take expert advice.

BUYING LAND

Foreigners cannot directly buy land that's located outside the urban perimeter and is classed as being Agricultural. However, in order to attract investors, the Moroccan Government has introduced a means by which you can change the legal nature of the land from

Agricultural to Residential. Investors need to apply for a VNA (Vocation Non Agricole), which is a complex procedure. The process for buying land is provided in detail below but, generally, if you are buying within an urban area, you will be able to proceed without a VNA; if you are buying outside of an urban area, in a rural or suburban zone, the chances are you will need to apply for a VNA.

Relevant authorities

The Land Registry (Conservation Foncière)

The Moroccan Land Registry office holds all the details on land history in the country, including the status of a title, the family who own the land and whether there are any outstanding debts held against the plot. All documentation will be in Arabic so it's recommended that any visit to the Land Registry is carried out with your notary. If the land is untitled (which, chances are, it will be) then you will have to obtain a title before you'll be allowed to buy and organise for the land registry to send a surveyor out to measure the plot, as with you would an untitled property.

Urban Agency (Commune Urbaine)

It is here that you will find out if there are any planned developments or construction works taking place near your potential plot of land, as plans will have been lodged with the Urban Agency. This is where you will also find out how the land is zoned, for example is it Agricultural or not.

Securing a VNA

Once you have chosen a plot of land and done the necessary background checks with the Land Registry and Urban Agency, then it's time to draw up an Accord de Principe to apply for a VNA. This needs to be done while working with an architect, as the Accord de

Principe is a detailed plan of what you intend to do with the land once you have bought it. Note that the Accord is not as detailed as the plans required to secure planning permission – this stage will come later (see Chapter 8).

The Accord must be submitted to the relevant commune for your area, who will then pass it to the regional committee and the Centres of Regional Investment (Centre Régionale d'Investissement). The approval process can take between one and two months and, once approved, you can continue with the purchasing process. Do not proceed until you have approval, and if you are obliged to sign a Preliminary Contract ensure that there is a conditional clause stating that the sale will only proceed if the VNA is granted. Once the VNA has been issued, your title secured and family members consulted regarding the sale, you can then proceed to completion.

BUYING A NEW BUILD

The Plan Azur program was introduced in 2001 by the Moroccan government in order to help reinvigorate tourism and investment into the country, and it has successfully given rise to many new property developments, especially in the north. Most estate agents in the UK are currently advertising the sale of off-plan rather than resale properties, at prices starting from as little as £32,000 (486,712 dirhams).

Buying off-plan is always attractive because the purchasing price is so much lower than the value of the property on completion, but there are risks involved that every investor should be aware of and you should always consult an independent legal adviser before signing any contract in Morocco.

Buying off-plan is slightly different to buying a resale property as there is a special law – the VEFA (Vente en l'Etat Future d'Achévement) – which was introduced in October 2002 in order to protect buyers from fraud and to put an end to 'black market' construction. This law is heavily protective of the buyer – for example, it forbids any payment to be made before the signature of the Preliminary Contract, which can only be drawn up by a notary or a Moroccan lawyer after the completion of the foundations. The developers also have to provide a bank guarantee in order to secure the purchaser's investments. Only when a potential buyer is happy with the Preliminary Contract should they sign and commit to buying from the developer.

The contract contains details on:

◆ Stage payments: the first payment is normally made on the completion of foundations; the second on completion of the main structure; and the third once the property is fully completed to the standard agreed in the VEFA.

◆ The full price of the property.

◆ The delivery schedule, for instance what part of the property will be completed when.

◆ A bank guarantee for the property price.

◆ Copies of the architect's plans.

◆ The documents confirming that building permission has been granted for construction.

◆ How payment will be made by the buyer.

◆ Certification from the engineers that the foundations have been completed.

This contract is always only signed once the foundations have been completed and the first stage payment is due. Always ensure that you are provided with a VEFA as this safeguards you against any financial loss and dodgy developers. This law is often criticised by developers in Morocco as being too harsh, and consequently some developers may not have a VEFA – if so, you should steer clear.

BUYING MULTIPLE PROPERTIES

Purchasing through a limited company

If you intend to purchase more than one Moroccan property, it may well be worth considering establishing a Moroccan Private Limited Company. The minimum equity capital is 10,000 dirhams (£660), and while the company can be formed by one person, it cannot exceed 50 in number.

Centres of Regional Investment (CRI)

If you are looking to purchase land or property in bulk, then you may well find yourself visiting your Centre of Regional Investment (CRI). CRIs were introduced in 2002 to help in the development and encouragement of foreign investment into Morocco, and essentially act as a go-between between a potential investor and the land owner/administrative departments related to the purchase of property and land. Each region has its own CRI which is responsible for investment and development within that area.

FINAL CHECKLIST

✓ Always establish a budget and stick to it.

✓ Always view the area and as many properties as possible before committing to buy, and consider renting in the area to get to know it better.

✓ Try to view a property you are considering buying at different times of day, throughout the year.

✓ Think twice before you buy – is the area right for you? Make sure the answer is yes before you sign the legally binding contract.

✓ Make sure that the property corresponds to its description in both the estate agent's details and the title in the Land Registry, and get your lawyer to carry out a thorough background check before purchasing.

149

✓ Make sure you're paying market value for the property and aren't the victim of overcharging, as foreigners in Morocco can be.

✓ Always check the additional costs of the purchase, such as taxes and fees for the notary, estate agent and lawyer.

✓ Make sure that planning permission has been granted for the property and that any future work you want to do will also be approved.

✓ Always clarify what is and what is not included in the sale, such as fittings and furnishings.

✓ Have any documentation translated into English before you sign it.

✓ Appoint a power of attorney to sign the Preliminary and Final Contracts on your behalf if you can't attend.

✓ Make sure that there are get-out clauses in the Preliminary contract for any issues such as the seller backing out or failure by the developer to complete an off-plan property.

✓ Never sign a document unless you know exactly what you're agreeing to.

✓ Be sure of any key dates or deadlines and adhere to them – missing a stage payment could lose you your property.

✓ Always use a professional to check that the paperwork relating to the property is in order.

✓ Have a survey done on the property and check the exact boundaries, clarifying all rights of way and access routes.

✓ Never buy from a developer who doesn't provide a VEFA.

✓ Always check the zoning of land before committing to buying.

7
Letting your property

BUY-TO-LET PROPERTIES

Morocco is undoubtedly one of the hottest buy-to-let markets at the moment, being only three hours from the UK, and with an exotic culture, fabulous climate and 3,500 km of coastline. Thanks to the government's focus on the development of the holiday industry and the new resorts that are springing up, tourism is destined to grow, especially as the Open Skies plan continues to make the country increasingly accessible. Morocco currently has a solid rental market with occupancy rates of around 85% during peak season and this is expected to rise as Plan Azur nears completion.

Approximately 4.3 million tourists visited Morocco in the first seven months of 2007, an increase of 10% on 2006, with over 1 million tourists visiting the country in July alone. The largest number of foreign visitors came from France (1.7 million), followed by visitors from Spain (795,000), Belgium (285,000), the UK (261,000), the Netherlands (211,000), Germany (182,000) and Italy (164,000). The Department of Tourism reported that the total number of nights spent in hotels increased by 7% for 2007, reaching 10 million.

The concept of buying a property in order to make money from letting it – i.e. buy-to-let – has become a massive phenomenon in recent years. The vast majority of people who purchase overseas buy with the intention of holidaying there for four to six weeks a year, and look to rent it out for the remaining time, a move which can help generate some welcome income to cover costs. As a UK resident you will have the benefit of being able to tap into the growing market of foreign rentals, as well as having an understanding of the needs and standards of furnishings that a foreign holidaymaker will expect, so you can market and furnish your home accordingly.

However, a word of warning. Many people think they can cover their entire mortgage costs simply by renting their property for a few weeks every year but this is very unlikely to happen. Yes, Morocco offers high rental yields and, yes, you can expect to secure a healthy rental income that will go a long way to helping you afford your home, but don't take the risk of relying solely on rental income to cover the costs of a mortgage, wear and tear, furnishings and marketing.

Insider info

Adam Cornwell, Managing Director of GEM Estates, explains why the Moroccan market rental will continue to grow in the coming years.

The popularity of Morocco will continue to increase as more of the Plan Azur projects are finalised and Mediterrania Saïdia nears completion. Up until recently people have been nervous about investing in the market, sitting on the fence on the issue of Morocco, but they have begun to better realise the concept and quality the market can offer. Also, the continued growth of tourism will fuel the demand for many years to come as rental accommodation becomes coveted. With all the 'emerging market' hype surrounding so many destinations, people have a misconception that markets such as Morocco will come and go overnight; that simply isn't the case. Morocco is here to stay and will continue to grow for many years to come, most notably because it is a large country with infinite appeal, from ski resorts to the coast and beaches, to the imperial cities. With King Mohammed at the helm, the only way is up and his focused and ambitious plan to attract 10 million tourists to the country by 2010 (from 5.8 million in 2005) is already on target.

International airport arrivals Jan–Sept 2007

Mohammed V, Casablanca: 3,643,000 (increase of 16% on 2006)
Marrakesh: 2,086,000 (increase of 22% on 2006)
Agadir: 870,000 (increase of 7% on 2006)
Rabat-Sale: 179,000 (increase of 18% on 2006)

Tangier: 221,000 (increase of 26% on 2006)
Fès: 177,000 (increase of 81% on 2006)
Oujda: 182,000 (increase of 25% on 2006)
Nador: 125,000 (increase of 55% on 2006)
Ouarzazate: 20,000 (increase of 1% on 2006)

SHORT- OR LONG-TERM?

Whatever you decide to do, if you intend to be reliant on rental income in order to make your investment a stable one then it is imperative that you closely examine the current and future state of the market and the location you plan to buy in. Talk to letting agencies and travel agents and ask them where they think the best investments are to be made. Any planned increase in budget flights is a good sign that the market will be opening up to tourists, providing you with future demand for short-term lettings. Take a look at what other rentals are available in a certain area, what people are charging, and how many weeks of rentals they can secure per year. These are all indicators that will help you to make an informed decision.

There are some locations in Morocco where you can secure long-term rentals – such as Casablanca, Tangier and Marrakesh – where there are substantial business communities and foreigners looking for a rental property while working in the city. While letting long-term will severely limit the time you can spend in your home, in the long run, it means the property is being looked after and you have a healthy and regular income generated from it.

However, short-term rentals are where the Moroccan market is at its strongest, with many new coastal developments springing up and an expansive coastline with established resorts such as Essaouira and the city of Marrakesh already drawing a healthy holiday market. The area around Agadir is also becoming increasingly popular and touted as the next big thing in holiday and tourist terms.

153

The benefits of renting short-term are that you can secure higher rental yields than you would for a long-term let, and you will also have access to and use of your property at certain times of the year. However, short-term rental properties do suffer from more wear and tear, and there are also the issues and costs of marketing, cleaning and maintenance – all things that need to be taken into consideration. In many cases, people are attracted by the novelty of staying in a traditional Moroccan property, and so if you are buying a riad to renovate, you can also expect to generate good rental returns from holiday-makers in places such as Fès and Marrakesh. Given Morocco's proximity to Europe, you can also tap into the weekend break crowd.

The pros and cons of renting

Pros

◆ You can make money to cover repayments.

◆ Your home will be occupied and cared for during your absence.

◆ You can employ a holiday letting company to do the hard work and marketing for you.

◆ You have secured a nest egg for the future.

◆ The Moroccan market is constantly growing, fuelled by media interest and the government's Plan Azur. The tourist board is reporting massive growth, with an 18% increase in 2007 on the number of holiday-makers visiting the country compared to the previous year.

Cons

◆ You may find that you cannot spend time in your home during peak or summer seasons as that's when you experience the most demand and make most money.

◆ You will need to employ the services of a maintenance and cleaning firm which can sap your income.

◆ You will need to look into tenancy legislation and tax payments.

◆ Furnishings and facilities have to be provided.

◆ The garden will need to be tended.

◆ If something breaks or there are problems then you may not be in the country to deal with them.

THE IMPORTANCE OF LOCATION

You may think it is a cliché, but that old adage 'location, location, location' will never wear thin in terms of choosing a property with the intention of letting. If you buy somewhere too far from the airport, you're unlikely to secure many lets. if you buy in 'no man's land' – i.e. desert or mountain areas – too far from the coast, ski resorts or major cities, then the likelihood is that very few people will show an interest. Buying a home to let has to be a business decision and, as such, you need to think very carefully about the location and put your own tastes to one side.

Choosing a location

The first thing to do is to ensure that the area you are looking to buy in is not saturated with rentals, as this minimises your chances of securing a healthy number of bookings. This doesn't mean you should pick an area which is virtually unknown – the best bet is to look at the newly developing areas where budget flights are fairly regular. That said, in Morocco demand is still very strong, and so you can still expect to see a healthy return even in the major tourist markets of Marrakesh and Essaouira, although areas such as Fès and Agadir may have a more promising future for investors as they are beginning to be discovered by many more people.

The next thing to do is get to know the area and see what kind of amenities and infrastructure are in place that will benefit your guests. The kind of facilities you are looking for obviously depends on whether you are trying to attract short- or long-term rents. Most holiday-makers will either want the property to have a pool and a large garden for barbecues, or to be near the beach, so be prepared to pay a little extra for a premium location. Proximity to the airport is a must as most people are generally not prepared to travel for more than 90 minutes to reach their rental accommodation. Look into the airports that are set to open or be redeveloped around the country, and pay particular attention to where budget flights are going. For example, the airport at Oujda is set to receive budget flights soon, serving the popular resort of Saïdia and having a positive effect on tourism and investment in the region.

Long-term renters will want to be close to supermarkets, their office and possibly schools if renting with their family. City centre apartments, close to the transport network, clubs, bars and restaurants are the prime locations.

Today it is even possible to buy a newly built property with guaranteed rental income for a fixed number of years. While this can be a good deal, be wary of taking a developer at their word and make sure you get proof and written confirmation before entering into a sale.

Where to buy

Marrakesh remains the most attractive tourist destination in Morocco, with a growth rate of 11%, followed by Casablanca (10%), Tangier (9%), Fès (7%), Rabat (6%) and Agadir (3%). As the number one destination for tourists to the country, Marrakesh is worth looking at in terms of rentals, as they are only destined to get higher – Marrakesh airport saw a 22% increase in arrivals in 2007 compared to 2006. Obviously, areas which are nominated Plan Azur resort locations are good options, along with cities such as Tangier and Casablanca, which are actively seeking to increase tourist figures.

Morocco has some 18 golf courses, and developments in and around these courses are becoming increasingly popular, especially as Morocco offers a fabulous year-round climate for golfers. From a rentals point of view these are also hot locations, with golfing holidays an expanding market. Currently there are three courses in Agadir, one in Benslimane, two in Casablanca, one in El Jadida, one in Fès, three in Marrakesh, one in Meknès, one in Mohammeidia, one in Ouarzazate, two in Rabat, one in Tangier and one in Tetouan.

In terms of where offers the best rental returns, figures are still hard to come by as the market is in the early stages of development, although on average, for a three-bedroom property (generally a riad) in Marrakesh and Essaouira, you can expect to generate around £690 a week. In Agadir you can command anything from £200 to £350 a week, rising to £1,000 to £1,500 for a luxury villa near the coast. In El Jadida prices are similar, with a three-bedroom self-catering villa with a traditional interior starting at £225, rising to £1,050 for a property on a golfing development. You can generate from £180 to £380 for a modern two-bedroom apartment in Tangier, while in Fès, a two-bedroom self-catering apartment in the Ville Nouvelle will secure you between £290 and £350. Along the Atlantic Coast and within the medinas, prices do rise for rentals, with £600 to £1,000 the charge during peak season, depending on the exact location and property type. For a more detailed look at locations, see Chapter 3.

SETTING A PRICE

When looking at how much to charge for rentals, firstly, you must think about whether you intend to make a living out of renting property or if you are just trying to cover your costs. For instance, you will be able to generate more income from the coastal resorts of Essaouira and Saïdia than you currently would from the ski resorts of the High Atlas. Similarly, if you are letting long-term, obviously you will be making less per week, but you'll have a guaranteed income over a longer period, so you need to calculate roughly what your income would be for the year.

The best thing to do is find out how much other properties of a similar size and in the same area are charging, allowing you to estimate the kind of income you can expect to generate. This is important, not only so that you don't price yourself out of the market, but so that if possible you could look to slightly undercut the competition, thus ending up securing more rentals and more money in the long run. Talk to rental agencies, pick up brochures and local papers, go online and look for rental properties in the area, and make sure you do your research thoroughly before setting a weekly rate. When you first start letting, you may also want to offer a special deal or discount in order to build up a client base and secure bookings.

Insider info

In order to assess whether renting your property will be a viable option, figure out how much income you will be likely to generate a week, and how many weeks worth of rentals you can generally expect per year. Divide the net annual rent by the value of the property and if you end up with a figure less than 6% or 7% then your property is not going to be a profitable buy-to-let investment.

FURNISHING THE PROPERTY

Regardless of where you buy and what the area can offer, if you don't furnish your property properly then you are unlikely to secure large numbers of bookings, and the prospect of re-bookings will be very low. This is just as important with long-term rentals, especially as you are probably going to be looking at renting to single businessmen or young couples, who will want a modern look and feel from their home.

The first rule is to make sure everything is clean and tidy and in working order. Ensure that all facilities, such as a television, fridge, freezer and cooker are in place and leave instructions on how to use them. Always make sure that there is fresh linen and towels in the property as no one wants to have to bring these in their luggage. The standard of your furnishings generally dictates how much you can charge, but be prepared for breakages and wear and tear – furniture should be hard-wearing and easy to clean. Bedrooms should have comfy beds and space for clothes to be hung, and providing a sofa bed in the living room will also allow you to up the rent charged, as you can provide accommodation for more people.

Added extras such as a washing machine or tumble dryer is always a good idea, along with beach equipment, such as windbreakers, surf/body boards, etc. It's recommended that air conditioning is available for the hot summer months and, if you can, put together an information pack on the area with details of things to do, attractions to see and the best places for food and drink. Providing dry supplies such as tea and coffee will also help make your guests feel more at home.

The general appeal for many people who holiday in Morocco is not only the weather but also the exotic nature of the country, so if you can offer a few traditional furnishings and touches, then this will help secure bookings and also build a base of clients for re-booking in the future.

MARKETING

If you intend to rent your property then you need to be prepared to spend some time and money on marketing it effectively. The first few years are always likely to be tough and little money will be made as it's spent on marketing and furnishings, but if you ensure you put the work in early on and spend time making your property feel welcoming and homely, then you are sure to build up a regular client base which will probably sustain you for the foreseeable future.

To start with, you need to get your property advertised and there are numerous ways of doing this. One of the best is to use a holiday lettings website. For a small fee – and in some cases no fee at all – you can upload details about your property online, allowing people to view and book via the internet. There are also numerous magazines and newspapers where you can place ads, and a wealth of property management companies that will handle all the marketing, booking details and cleaning of the property for you.

If you intend to let your property then it's probably sensible to set up a dedicated email address and phone number, especially if you don't want to publicise your home phone number. There are also a number of cheap and easy packages that enable you to set up your own website – for example, www.1and1.com.

If you decide to market your own home, be prepared to do the following:

◆ Follow up on queries straight away.

◆ Check your email and phone messages daily.

◆ Advertise, but make sure you do your research and advertise in the right medium, depending on the type of tenant you are trying to attract.

◆ Think about having your own brochure printed and do a yearly mail out to previous tenants.

◆ Make contacts in the local area and arrange an advertising deal with them – in return, you could recommend them to your clients.

◆ Advertise your property by word of mouth back in the UK. There are always rentals to be secured by sending emails around at work or getting friends to recommend your property.

◆ Keep an inventory of the contents of the property so you know if anything has been broken, damaged or stolen.

Insider info

Sarah Chambers of holiday-rentals.co.uk explains how to successfully let your home.

Always try to buy a property that stands out from the crowd, such as a riad or a property with traditional Moroccan features – its unique nature will encourage rentals.

When marketing, be aggressive in promoting your property. You can either use a reputable agent or do it yourself to avoid their fees. The internet is the first port of call for the majority of travellers, so this is the best channel to use. If you can't build your own website, you can use a holiday rentals website, such as www.Holiday-Rentals.co.uk, which includes free promotion on 12 international websites in its yearly subscription. Adverts are easy to set up and sites like this invest a lot of money in marketing to ensure they appear at the top of internet search results for holiday rental accommodation.

Once travellers find your property, it must make an impact. Keep furnishings simple and provide basics such as linen, towels, hairdryers and adapters. Take good-quality pictures to help sell your property – ideally you should include an exterior shot, photos of all rooms, outside areas (including pools) and, if possible, the view. Include detailed descriptions of the property and surrounding area to showcase all that's on offer and to set the holiday scene. For your guests' arrival, ensure you provide a comprehensive guide to the area. Finally, extras that may help give you an edge could include airport pick-ups, a car, or a welcome pack with some local specialities and wine, all included in the price.

USING A MANAGEMENT COMPANY

If you don't feel you have the time or expertise to manage the letting of your property, then you can employ a property management company to do it for you. This is especially handy if you intend to remain in the UK. Generally speaking, if you manage the letting of your property yourself, you have the opportunity to generate more income and be more successful in securing rentals. This is simply because you will be giving the project your undivided attention, unlike most management companies who have a large number of clients on their books and generally charge a fairly hefty rate of commission.

Nevertheless, a decent company will be able to take care of the marketing, maintenance, client liaison and booking of the property, and deal with all the bureaucracy and red tape that might come with the territory, making them value for money if they are good at their job. While most will be able to generate a large number of rentals during peak season, you need to be aware that they will have other clients on their books, so you won't get priority treatment. Also, don't take promises of year-round bookings and hefty yearly yields too seriously, as in reality this is unlikely to happen.

Costs vary, although you are normally looking at up to 20% of your earnings. Make sure you tie them down on their promises and get

BUYING A PROPERTY IN MOROCCO

guarantees about the number of weeks of rentals and level of income to expect. Finding a decent company isn't always easy, although your estate agent should be able to recommend someone to you, and word of mouth recommendations are always a good starting point. However, if you are not going to be based in Morocco, it may well pay to have someone based in the same country as you to avoid being scammed and to make communication easier.

LEGAL ISSUES

If you intend to let your property then the best starting point is to make sure you notify the authorities in the relevant region that you will be doing so. You should also brush up on local tenancy laws and take legal advice.

Generally speaking you will be taxed on your rental income in the country where the income was earned, i.e. where your rental property is located. Income tax is charged at a progressive rate as follows, although new buyers are exempt from property rental tax for the first five years they rent their home.

Annual income/Rent in DH	Rate
Up to 24,000	0%
24,001–30,000	15%
30,001–45,000	25%
45,001–60,000	35%
60,001–120,000	40%
More than 120,001	42%

8
Building and renovating

If you decide that you want to build your dream home in Morocco, or even renovate a run-down traditional property, then you need to be aware that these are not simple, straightforward things to do. While it can be difficult in the UK, never mind Spain and Italy where red tape abound, in Morocco you will face problems of a slightly different ilk, so be prepared to be patient, and to employ the best possible people to help you realise your dream. Remember, while levels of craftsmanship may be good in Morocco, structural buildings aren't always up to standard, so you need to make sure you get experienced builders and engineers involved.

Bear in mind that the price of land in Morocco has trebled over the past five years, fuelled by the increased interest and demand for development in the country, so depending on where you want to build, the initial cost of land might be higher than you realise for such an immature market.

OBTAINING A BUILDING PERMIT

Before you decide to go ahead with any kind of facelift or major building work, you are required to secure a building permit (Rokhsat al Binaa). These can be secured from the Urban or Rural Commune (Jema'a) and are required for all of the following:

◆ Changing of the garden/garden path layout.

◆ Moving or putting up fencing.

♦ Building from scratch.

♦ Knocking down walls or changing a building's interior layout.

♦ Changing the external appearance of a building.

♦ Structural renovation or restoration.

Bear in mind that obtaining this permit will take time, and may also result in the plans being sent back to you to be 'tweaked' before you get the permission you are looking for. In order to submit planning permission, you will have to employ an architect to draw up any plans for building, restoration or conversion. These plans will be verified and checked against the zoning regulations – be aware that restrictions may apply to the area you are looking to build in. For example, if you apply to build a four-storey house in an area only zoned for two storeys then the Urban Commune will be involved, although this does not automatically mean your application will get turned down.

If you are looking to buy a plot of land to build on which is zoned for Agricultural usage, prior to the purchase and application for planning, you will need to secure a VNA to transfer the lands usage to Residential – see Chapter 6 on The Buying Process for more details. As mentioned above, it is worth checking all the zoning details prior to your purchase so you can see if you are likely to be able to secure planning permission for the build you want to pursue. For example, in urban areas the house may only be allowed to be a certain size depending on the size of the plot purchased, or you may have to buy at least one hectare of land in another area. These are all key things to research before you look to buy and build.

Generally you will find the approval process takes between two and thee months and costs around £1.32 (20 dirhams) per square metre of build in building tax. Once your architect's plans have been stamped – this is the approval needed to go ahead with the build – then you can start work, although you must do so within one year, or else your permission will expire.

Once you have finalised your restoration or building work, then you will need to secure a Cerificat de Conformité from your architect, which states that the work complies to the building regulations submitted. You must then notify the Commune that the build has finished and the certificate issued, and they will send a representative out to view the work. If they are satisfied, you will be issued with a Permis d'Habitation stating that the property is ready to be lived in and complies with the regional regulations and submitted plans.

VAT

If your property has been newly built and covers an area larger than 240 square metres, you will have to pay tax on the building materials and labour. Keep all receipts to prove what you have spent and that VAT has already been paid on it, otherwise you will be charged a flat rate of 20% for building services and 14% for any materials used.

RENOVATING

The major problem with buying and renovating in Morocco comes down to the issue of titles – old properties that have been around for hundreds of years and have had multiple owners require your notary to carry out the arduous task of securing approval for the sale from all family members.

The cost of renovation is also expensive and, while it varies, on average you are looking at around 50% of the property price. Local labour is not generally the issue, although it is in high demand which may make it hard to find a reputable builder. The main costs involved in renovating are simply associated with sourcing and buying the right kind of materials to renovate your property.

What you can and can't do in terms of renovations depends on where the property is located and how protected it is. Whether or not you can pull down internal walls depends on the style, location and age of the building, yet in some suburbs of Marrakesh you will find homes which have walls built from mud, so nobody really minds what you do with them. Either way, the most important aspect of renovating is to make sure you plan costs down to the last possible detail, always have a contingency budget and ensure you know exactly what you are allowed to build. That way, you can avoid any nasty surprises.

BUILDING

As with any country in the world, building your own home is likely be a stressful, costly and time-consuming business. Moroccan builders, while exceptionally good at their jobs and surprisingly cheap, can be just as unreliable as any other builders. That said, it is always best to employ Moroccan artisans because they know the best local materials to use and the regional styles, so they can build in a sympathetic style. They are also cheaper than bringing in foreign builders.

There are always problems to be faced, such as the language barrier, red tape and the time required to successfully complete a build. While all of these can be eased by using an experienced team of professionals, you also have to look at the practicalities of taking on a new-build. To start with, there are the costs. Always get an accurate quote for the entire project prior to signing any agreements with builders or architects. Shop around, ask several people, look at the price of materials and the cost of local furnishings. Make a list of every little detail and fitting the building will need, down to the tiniest screw, as this is the best way to estimate the overall costs. Once you have reached your final figure, factor in a contingency budget, which should be about 15% on top of your estimate – you never know what you may have overseen or what can go wrong.

Don't be tempted to go along the unofficial, and admittedly cheaper, route of not drawing up plans and allowing your builder to work without the officially stamped planning permission – the authorities are cracking down and you may end up having your property demolished. In terms of what you do with the exterior of the property, remember that in coastal areas such as Essaouira, the colour scheme is white and blue, while in Marrakesh it's red.

EMPLOYING PROFESSIONALS

You can't beat experience, especially when you are looking to build a new home in a foreign country and have little knowledge of the bureaucracy or the language. So whatever you do, always hire the best!

Architects

You are obliged to hire an architect, at the very least in order to secure planning permission – the architect will need to draw up the plans to submit to the local Commune. You can choose either to hire an architect for your whole build or renovation, or simply to draw up the plans and then allow your builder to take control. However, you must have a Moroccan architect involved in the process in order to sign off the plans. You can't simply employ a European architect to do the job – they would need to work with a Moroccan professional.

While it will obviously be more expensive to secure the services of an architect for the whole build – 5 to 8%, depending on your requirements – it will offer more peace of mind, especially if you won't be in the country for the duration of the build.

When agreeing a price with your architect for their work, remember that they will ask for a percentage of the total build cost, so ensure that it isn't too high in relation to the cost of the total build. Always get an agreed quote in writing and secure a contract with your architect which details the kind of work they will be undertaking for you. If necessary, your architect can hold power of attorney for you if he will be overseeing the work while you are out of the country. At the very least, your architect should:

◆ Draw up plans for the build.

◆ Draw up the Cahier des Prescriptions Speciale – this details the kind of materials that will be used and all the work that will be carried out on the build.

◆ Oversee the build and manage the builders (payments, etc.).

◆ On completion, sign the Certificat de Conformité.

If you are going to be giving your architect responsibility for the construction of your dream home then you need to be confident in them. Consequently, when you are looking for an architect, always ask to see their certification, try to secure an objective recommendation and always ask to see some of their work. And remember, a big firm isn't necessarily better than a smaller one.

In terms of finding a good architect, the Moroccan Society of Architects includes all formally qualified architects in the country, and so is a good starting point. As always, recommendations from friends, family and your estate agent could be invaluable too.

Builders

One of the key aspects of working with Moroccan builders is to always expect everything to take longer than anticipated – there's very much a mañana attitude – as the Moroccan people will always put family before work, and are strong believers in the preordained – i.e. fate dictates when your build will be completed, not the builder! Builders will be keen to work for you, as in Moroccan terms you will be paying them well – or at least, more than they would get for local work. Ensure that you get an estimate (dervis) for all works, and include everything when drawing up a contract, from buying nuts and bolts to clearing up the site and putting up the walls. If you don't, you could find you are constantly being asked for extra hand-outs to cover costs.

One of the most shocking aspects of hiring local builders is that many will actually live in the building while working for you, simply because they may have come from out of town to work on your property. Don't worry, this is a normal occurrence!

Always hire a building contractor or architect to oversee the works for you – unless, of course, you feel confident enough to manage them yourself. Your building contractor will be able to source plumbers, electricians and all the additional manpower you will require, so in many ways this is the best way to progress with your build. Even if you do employ a contractor to organise things, make sure you visit the site regularly and check on the quality of the construction and materials being used. As with all your workers, draw up a contract with the building contractor and expect to pay between £150 and £200 per square metre for their involvement.

Structural engineers

As well as requiring the services of an architect, you may well find you need a structural engineer too – contact the local CRI for recommendations. They will check all the plans to make sure that the building's structure is correct and they'll need to rubber stamp the plans in order to get them approved, ensuring that building permission is granted.

Artisans

Moroccan artisans are among the best in the world and they can add some wonderful touches to your property. Most still employ traditional methods dating back hundreds of years, and they are in demand. They are the ones who will transform the shell of your house into a stunning new home, and they can fit tiles, shape doorways and much more. When looking to find an artisan, you can either use recommended craftsman or go looking for them yourself – some have workshops in town.

169

Always be specific about what you want from your interior, providing samples, photographs and sketches. Artisans will also happily take on commissions for you, such as creating bespoke furniture. If you are buying a riad to restore or a traditional property, always try to use a skilled artisan as this way not only will you end up producing a property which is sympathetic with the local area, but you will also have a home with the sort of local features – tiles, mosaics, ironwork, colours – that will attract tourists looking for an authentic holiday property.

Alternatively, if you are keen to go along the more modern route, then Morocco does have an Ikea-esque superstore called Kitea, which offers a range of furnishings and fittings.

9
Relocating yourself and your family

The decision to move yourself and your family overseas is never an easy one and moving is always a stressful time, whether you're going just down the road or all the way to Morocco! The best advice is to be prepared. If you try to plan ahead and think of every little obstacle, no matter how obscure, then you'll get through it fine; remember, just be organised!

VISAS, RESIDENCY AND PERMITS

Tourist/visitor visas

As a UK citizen, there is no need to apply for a visa to enter Morocco. As long as you have a return ticket and a passport that is valid for six months from your entry date, then you can stay for three months without a visa.

All citizens of EU member states as well as Australians, Canadians, Americans and Japanese, may also stay for up to three months on their passport, as can nationals of Algeria, Andorra, Argentina, Bahrain, Brazil, Chile, Congo, Côte d'Ivoire, Guinea, Iceland, Indonesia, Korea, Kuwait, Libya, Liechtenstein, Mali, Mexico, Monaco, New Zealand, Niger, Norway, Oman, Peru, The Philippines, Puerto Rico, Qatar, Russian Federation, Saudi Arabia, Senegal, Singapore, Switzerland, Tunisia, Turkey, United Arab

Emirates and Venezuela. Nationals of Hong Kong can stay in Morocco without a visa for up to 30 days.

Types of visa and cost

Visas for short visits are generally issued as either a Moroccan tourist visa (also known as the visit visa, visitor visa or travel visa) or a Moroccan business visa, also known as the business visit visa. In practice, both visas are valid for the same duration, but the requirements for each differ slightly.

A single-entry visa costs £16, while a double-entry or multiple-entry (both business only) will set you back £25. Prices can fluctuate with the exchange rate and may be paid by postal order only. Entry visas are valid for three months and visitors wishing to stay longer should apply to the local police station within 15 days of their arrival in Morocco.

Moroccan tourist visa

Moroccan tourist visas are designed for those who wish to take a holiday in Morocco or want to enter the country for a short period of time to visit family and friends. A tourist visa for Morocco is issued for a duration of three months and, like equivalent tourist visas in destinations across the world, this type of permit is a temporary solution. People entering Morocco through a permit of this type are obliged to return to their country of residence at the end of their time in Morocco and are not permitted to undertake employment in the country.

Moroccan business visa

Moroccan business visas are also issued for a duration of three months, although they can be granted as either a single entry or multiple entry permit. In Morocco, business visas are designed for those who wish to visit the country in order to engage in business activities, rather than those seeking fulltime employment in Morocco.

There are also student, employment, and permanent residency visa forms available, depending on your requirements and intentions in the country.

Applying for a visa

In order to apply for a visa you should provide the following:

- One completed application form which you can download from http://embassyhomepage.com/morocco

- Four passport-size photos taken within the previous six months.

- Valid passport with at least one blank page, and with a photocopy of the relevant data pages.

- Fee, payable by postal order only (see information above).

- Photocopy of all flight bookings.

- Photocopy of hotel reservation.

- Letter from employer or educator.

- Self-addressed, stamped, registered envelope for postal applications (for those living outside London only).

Upon receipt of all necessary documents, it normally takes four working days to process a visa, although some nationals should note that their application forms are sent to Morocco for clearance and processing and may take up to two months.

Useful contacts

Embassy of the Kingdom of Morocco in the UK
49 Queen's Gate Gardens, London SW7 5NE, UK
Tel: 020 7581 5001/4
Website: www.mincom.gov.ma
Opening hours: Mon–Fri 9.30 am–5 pm; Saturday 10 am–1 pm (visa section); closed UK and Moroccan national holidays (see page 220 for details on these) and open until 3 pm during Ramadan.

Moroccan Consulate in the UK
Diamond House, 97–99 Praed Street, London W2 1NT, UK
Tel: 020 7724 0624
Opening hours: Mon–Fri 9 am–12.30 pm.

Residence permits

You can stay in Morocco for up to three months with your British passport. However, if you wish to stay in the country for longer than the three-month period you must apply for a visa extension within 15 days of your arrival. This is done by applying for an extension from the Foreign Registration Department (Service des Etrangers) of the local police station. If you wish to become a resident, you need to apply for a residential permit (Carte de séjour) from the local police station. Once received, the card is valid for ten years. This needs to be done in Morocco, once you have entered the country on a tourist visa. A Carte de séjour allows you to secure free education and healthcare.

Work permits

In Morocco, work permit applications are employer-led and may only be granted to candidates who have been offered a specific position with a particular Moroccan company. The company in question must apply on behalf of the candidate and will be required to demonstrate that the position being offered could not have been filled by a Moroccan citizen or permanent resident, and therefore has been offered to you instead.

Processing times and fees

Visa applications can often be processed within five working days. However, immigration visa services are frequently subject to change and may be affected by the type of entry clearance being pursued and the nationality of the applicant. In some circumstances, applications may take up to two months to process. Fees may also differ according to circumstance but, at present, entry visas cost between £16 and £25 depending upon whether they are issued on a single or multiple entry basis.

REMOVALS

Planning and preparation are the two most important things to bear in mind when moving overseas – see the checklist on page 178 to help you organise your move. Some people choose to drive themselves and their possessions into Morocco, piling everything into a van and travelling down through France and Spain. Alternatively, there are a number of removals companies that will take your personal effects over to Morocco. Think carefully about what you do take as in many cases your Western European furnishings could end up feeling out of place in a traditional Moroccan property.

If you decide that you do want to use a removals company, always get a number of quotes from different agencies as they can vary considerably. Generally speaking, you should be looking at between £2,000 and £4,000, but allow for extras – such as customs duty and insurance – on top of this.

You are entitled to take your personal effects and furniture into Morocco without any customs duties being payable, although you need to have obtained your residency permit beforehand, with Change of Residence stamped in the country where you were living and legalised at the Moroccan embassy. You'll need to send an inventory with your personal effects, which will be duty free provided they are older than six months; if they are new, you'll need to have receipts to accompany them and you'll have to pay duty. Allow between 16 and 32 days for your belongings to travel from the UK, get through customs and make it to your new property.

Obviously there will be restrictions on items that can be brought into the country – for example, weapons, drugs, explosives, Moroccan currency – and you should use your common sense. However, be

175

aware that you may need to pay duty on antique items, electrical items and items less than six months old. There are also limits on the amount of alcohol, medication, food and firearms (you need a licence) that can be imported.

You will need the following documentation to transport your belongings through customs:

◆ Inventory of shipment.

◆ Proof of property/tenancy agreement.

◆ Residence permit.

◆ Photocopy (in colour) of your passport.

Top tip
To save money, and if you aren't moving all your household furnishings, you could consider using a shared container service, which is a cost-effective method of shipping smaller loads overseas. Shipping costs are calculated on the amount of volume in cubic metres that your packed goods will take up in a 20-foot shipping container. To calculate your cubic metre volume you simply multiply the length x width x height in metres. Most companies offer this – see page 211 for contact details.

IMPORTING YOUR CAR

You are entitled to bring your motor vehicle into Morocco for a period of six months with temporary admission via document D161, but you need to make sure you either have insurance that covers Morocco or purchase insurance as you enter the country. Once your six months is up, you either need to apply for permanent admission or leave the country – a short jaunt to Spain will do it – and then re-enter Morocco on a D161 again. Insurance documentation (carte verte) can be bought from ports and entry points into Morocco.

If you decide to try to secure permanent admission, be aware that few people import their car into Morocco as duties and taxes are very high. You will also need to have secured a residence permit.

Duties and taxes amount to 59.25% of the car's value, with a discount of between 10% and 25%, depending on the age of the car. To secure permanent admission, you will need the following documentation:

◆ Residence permit.

◆ International driver's licence/EU licence.

◆ Receipt for purchase if your car is less than three years old.

◆ Temporary admission permit.

◆ Vehicle registration document.

TAKING YOUR PETS

If you simply can't move without taking your cat or dog with you, then there are certain steps you have to take that will allow you to move your pet on a passport without them being quarantined. You can get all the information you need from DEFRA. Your pet will need:

◆ An export health certificate 3916EHC, signed by a DEFRA vet.

◆ A rabies vaccination at least 30 days prior to departure, but no more than 12 months from departure.

◆ To have been resident in the UK for at least six months prior to the move.

◆ To be clear of any notable diseases within 48 hours of leaving UK.

◆ To be microchipped.

If you intend to return to the UK from Morocco with your pet, then you will need an importation licence. However, you'll have to leave them in quarantine for six months. DEFRA have a list of registered quarantine kennels.

RELOCATING WITH YOUR FAMILY

If your family are moving with you, there are several things to consider. You need to think about the quality of the education system, the kind of lifestyle your family would have and the impact living in an Islamic community would have upon them – would you be living among the local people, or within a foreign/expat environment? To help things go smoothly, take your family over to the area you will be living in and let them get a feel for the place prior to moving. Ensure your children have email accounts set up so they can continue to communicate with friends back home and, before the move, set up a calendar counting down the days, buy guidebooks and maybe even stick postcards of Morocco up around the house. Another idea is to try cooking some typical Moroccan foods at home before moving. Making sure that your family is educated and aware of what to expect is the most important thing, as this will help to ease the initial shock of relocating.

Language issues are always a problem, but most children learn French in school, so encourage them to put in some extra study to help with the transition. Adults should also try to learn basic words and phrases in French – the easiest of the Moroccan languages to master.

RELOCATION CHECKLIST

Five to six weeks before moving

✓ Ensure all the family's passports and visas are valid and up to date and check whether you will need to apply for work permits, residency permits or a driver's licence.

✓ Collate all necessary travel documentation and tickets for the journey abroad, as well as personal documents such as birth certificates, medical records (you need to obtain these from your GP) and marriage certificates.

✓ Set up a mail redirection service with the post office (www. postoffice.co.uk).

✓ Notify your children's schools and advise your solicitor, bank, doctor, dentist, insurance company and building society of your move, along with any creditors.

✓ Secure quotes for the removal of your items abroad.

✓ Ensure you have found suitable rental accommodation in Morocco (if necessary) and find a school for your child/children.

✓ Hand in your notice at work and arrange for any references you may need.

Three to four weeks to go

✓ Cancel all subscriptions to newspapers, clubs and magazines, and any club cards you may have.

✓ You will need to keep hold of all invoices for new purchases in order to import them through customs.

✓ Get copies of repeat prescriptions.

✓ Have a clear out and get rid of any unnecessary items, either by taking them to charity shops, having a car boot sale or by selling them online. Try eBay (www.ebay.co.uk) of Freecycle (www.uk.freecycle.org).

✓ Compile an inventory of all items that you will be transporting to your new home.

✓ Arrange with your utility providers to have all services disconnected on the day of your departure and try to ensure that all utilities are connected in your new home.

✓ Arrange for someone in the UK to be used as a contact point for any outstanding queries/bills and supply your new contact details to the relevant people/companies.

✓ Pay any debtors and cancel any rental agreements.

✓ Begin to run down all your stocks of food and drink.

✓ Confirm your removal date and decide which items you will pack, and begin to collect packing materials.

✓ Make a list of names, addresses and numbers you will need or want to remember, including any local businesses.

✓ Make arrangements to move your pets and secure a Pet Passport (see www.defra.gov.uk).

One to two weeks to go

✓ Clean and empty garden sheds and clean garden tools and bicycles that you want to take with you – they must be clean for importing.

✓ Arrange for mains services to be disconnected.

✓ Let newsagents and milkmen know your day of departure and pay their final accounts.

✓ Clear out school lockers and desks at work.

✓ Return any items you have loaned out or retrieve any you have lent to friends and family.

✓ Dispose of plants and perishable food.

✓ Finalise travel arrangements and get your car MOT'd and serviced if you are driving abroad.

✓ Correctly dispose of any flammables and white goods.

✓ If moving your TV antenna or satellite dish, make arrangements to have it taken down.

✓ Transfer bank and savings accounts and ensure you have access to funds abroad.

✓ Begin packing!

✓ Have the house thoroughly cleaned, including carpets. If you are taking any rugs or curtains with you, have these cleaned and packaged in protective bags.

✓ Cancel any unnecessary direct debits.

On to two days to go

✓ Pack all items you will need during your journey and when you get to your destination separately to those that are going to be shipped, such as keys, passports, tickets, clothes, money.

✓ Disconnect and clean any electrical appliances that you are taking with you.

✓ Pack a box of things you'll need as soon as you arrive and ensure it is packed at the entrance of the removal van so it will be the first thing off.

✓ Say your goodbyes and have a leaving party!

On moving day

✓ Leave enough food for breakfast/packed lunches. Invest in some plastic cutlery and paper plates.

✓ Make a list of things to check before you leave, such as cupboards, garage, loft and so on. Check the house to see if there is any damage – for example, floors or walls.

✓ Never leave before the removals company as they may have questions.

✓ Triple check that you have passports and travel documents.

Ticklist of people to notify

✓ Family and friends.

✓ Work colleagues.

✓ GP and dentist.

✓ Gym or fitness club.

✓ Insurance companies.

✓ DVLA.

✓ Banks and building societies.

✓ Utiltity companies (gas, electric, water, oil, telephone, internet).

✓ Inland Revenue.

✓ School/college/nightclass.

✓ Council.

✓ Newspaper/magazine subscription department.

✓ Clubs and organisations.

✓ Vet.

✓ Milkman.

✓ Cable provider.

✓ Church/place of worship.

✓ Credit card or loan company.

✓ Landlord (if renting).

✓ Tenants (if renting property anywhere).

10
Living in Morocco

The lifestyle in Morocco is going to be very different from what you are used to in Europe, so make sure you look into all aspects of living and working in the country before you leave home.

DAILY LIFE AND PEOPLE

There are many contrasts within Moroccan society, not least of all the Arabic/Berber and Muslim/European divide – indeed, this is a microcosm for what's taking place on a larger level, with Morocco rapidly integrating into the Western world. Moroccans are multilingual and multicultural, embracing not only a variety of languages – French and Arabic being the main two – but also new cultures, with the young particularly drawn to the Western European lifestyle.

To Moroccans, the focal point of life is the family, and everything else is subordinate to this. Other than family, the greatest influence on a Moroccan's life is Islam, which is an all-powerful, pervasive force that pretty much dictates the schedule of Moroccan life. That said, Morocco is one of the most liberal of the Arabic Islamic countries, with women happily pursuing their careers and living by themselves – although this is generally in the larger cities – and Western influences tolerated and even welcomed. Generally speaking, the people of Morocco are positive and forward-thinking. Generous and friendly, they're also very hospitable and will readily invite you into their home for a meal, especially if you are living alone, which to a Moroccan will be regarded with disbelief as well as pity.

One noteworthy aspect of Moroccan life is that of fatalism – essentially, the belief that what will be will be, as things are preordained by Allah. Consequently, aspects of Moroccan life, such as the massive and growing gulf between rich and poor, are accepted by most as just being the way things are – although that doesn't mean to say your average Moroccan isn't scathing towards the wealthy. The gulf between the town and the country is also rather stark, with the cities being modern, progressive and Westernised, and the rural areas of Morocco still very traditional and basic, home to poverty and hotbed of folklore.

COST OF LIVING

The cost of living in Morocco is between six to ten times cheaper than in the UK, and as a foreigner in Morocco you will be regarded as a wealthy person – and relatively speaking, you will be. Items such as food and alcohol are around 30% to 35% cheaper than in the UK, with souks selling fresh produce for low prices. Remember, though, that you should never accept the first price offered to you which will be far too high – always barter and generally bring the price down by one third. Bartering is part of Moroccan society and is expected of you, rather than frowned upon, so make sure you oblige.

The cost of labour is cheap and so DIY is unheard of, as your average Moroccan can generally afford to get someone to carry out any required building work for them.

UTILITIES

Depending on where and what you buy, you may find that you have no utilities connected. Generally speaking, buildings tend to have water and electricity connections, but few have a phone line installed. Don't expect to find gas connections as gas isn't piped in the country; instead, it is purchased in canisters.

Water

In the towns and cities water is almost universally safe to drink, and although some people prefer to use bottled water, there is no real necessity for this. However, in rural areas not all of the population receive mains water, with many still using wells, and in some cases those who do have access simply can't afford to connect to it. The government is aiming to rectify this and has a program in place (known as PAGER) to tackle the problem. Thanks to this scheme, 77% of the population now have water access.

ONEP (The National Office of Portable Water) is responsible for drinking-water production in Morocco, and although it distributes to some areas a municipally owned consortium normally oversees much of the population's supply, with some private companies operating in certain areas. Water prices are centrally controlled by the government (a situation which is likely to change), although private organisations can charge their own rates – this only affects the cities of Casablanca, Rabat, Tangier and Tetouan.

If your house already has water connected you will still need to ensure that you transfer the account into your name so that bills are addressed to you – the same is required if you need your supply turned on. To get connected you need to visit your local RAD (Regie Autonome de la Distribution de l'Eau and l'Electricité) – or RADEEF as they are commonly known – or ONEP building. Here, you'll have to show your Carte de séjour or passport, and either your Permis d'Habitation or Acte de Vente. You will generally be billed once every three months.

Electricity

Surprisingly, the cost of electricity in Morocco isn't that much lower than in the UK, with the National Electricity Office holding the monopoly on supplies. Morocco has been working hard to improve electricity coverage in the country, and by the end of 2006 it was estimated that around 90% of the rural population had access to electricity – up from 18% in 1995. There have also been a number of renewable energy projects launched in Morocco, with the National Electricity Office and Spanish wind turbine generator Gamesa beginning construction of a wind turbine park in Tangier in 2006, which aims to be operational in 2009.

Many of the houses in Morocco's medinas only have a 110V capacity, rather than the 220V needed to run most modern appliances. While you can buy a transformer, these have limited capabilities and can be easily overloaded. Therefore, the best method is to have the voltage changed to 220V – this will probably require you to update all the wiring in the house, so make sure you consult an electrician.

In order to transfer your voltage you will need to visit your local RADEEF and ask them to switch your capacity from 110V to 220V. For this you will need to produce:

◆ A photocopy of your passport.

◆ A copy of your previously paid bill (this will contain all of your electricity account details).

◆ 70 dirhams for the cost of switching.

It will then take a couple of weeks to get a new meter installed, which will allow you to run at a 220V capacity.

If you already have a 220V system, once you have bought your house all you will need to do is contact your electricity supplier in order to get the account transferred to your name. It is important to do this as quickly as possible in order to avoid incurring any unpaid debts left by the previous owner.

If the previous owner has had the power disconnected, you will need to get reconnected. In both instances this requires you to take your passport/Carte de séjour and the deeds of sale for your house to the regional authority (RADEEF) and arrange for a connection – this can take anything from 24 hours to a week to happen. It will cost around £11. Be aware that if you are taking British goods over to Morocco, you will need a European plug adapter as two-pin plugs are used there, as opposed to the UK three-pin system.

Gas

As there is no piped gas in Morocco, if you do want or need to use it you will need to purchase bottled butane or a propane canister known as Butagaz. In many cases this is recommended for things like heating water or powering a cooker, simply because it is more cost effective. Gas can be bought in bottles, which only need to be refilled once empty, that cost around £10. Most appliances need their own bottle, although you can power two appliances that are located close together by using a branching hose.

Gas is incredibly flammable and can be highly dangerous, so remember to be very careful when using it, and buy a regulator to control the gas pressure. Make sure there is ventilation in the area of the canister and if you are in any way anxious about gas leaking, switch the supply off. Finally, never store anything flammable or light a naked flame near your gas canister.

Telephone

There are many more mobile phone users than people with landlines in Morocco, and this is down to the limited availability of landlines as well as cost. If you are moving into a modern property in a Ville Nouveau, chances are you already have a working telephone line. If not, and there is one nearby, it will cost around 1,500 dirhams to get connected to it.

If there is no telephone provision in your area then you will need to approach ONPT (Office National de Postes et Télecommincations, www.onpt.net.ma – essentially Maroc Telecom) and arrange for an account to be opened for you; the amount of time this takes can vary considerably. Opening an account will require you to visit the office with the usual house deeds and passport/Carte de séjour.

Basic tariffs range from 0.33 dirhams a minute, with line rental of 96 dirhams per month. You will also have to pay an installation fee. You will be billed every month for your usage, with line rental paid in advance and calls made during the previous month added to that.

Mobile phones

If you are buying a house in Morocco or even just visiting, it is certainly worthwhile getting a pay-as-you-go sim card. These are available in most teleboutiques (essentially a public payphone shop) and cost about 50 dirhams. Most foreigners simply use a mobile phone rather than worrying about getting a landline installed. If you have been living in Morocco for longer than 12 months then you could get a contract with one of Morocco's mobile phone companies, which will cost around £12 a month with calls on top. Tariffs vary from 12p per minute to 56p per minute. The largest providers are Maroc Telecom (www.onpt.net.ma) and Meditel (www.meditel.ma).

Internet

You'll find numerous internet cafes throughout Morocco and a growing number of ISPs (internet service providers). If you are planning on using the internet at home then you will need to be connected as in the UK, and the process is pretty much the same as organising a telephone connection. You will need the usual passport/ Carte de séjour and house deeds to prove your address, as well as proof that you have a line installed with Maroc Telecom. You then fill in a contract as with your landline, and you will have the choice of a 12-month (520 dirham installation fee) or 24-month (270 dirham installation fee) contract. Bandwidth tariffs vary from 128kbps (199 dirhams per month), right up to 1,024kbps (499 dirhams per month). You will be given an installation pack with your modem, a software CD, ADSL filters and all your cables. If your phone line is already installed, as in the UK, there will be no need for an engineer to visit.

INSURANCE

There is no obligation to secure house insurance in Morocco unless you have a mortgage, in which case you will need to insure against natural disaster and fire, as well as obtaining life insurance for yourself. Companies in the UK such as AssetSure (www.assetsure. com) offer insurance for your holiday home in Morocco, as does John Wason (www.johnwason.co.uk).

You should also take out private health insurance as there is little money spent on the national healthcare system by the government and standards can be poor. Worldwide organisations such as AXA are probably your best bet and they have an office in Morocco and can deal with all your insurance needs. Visit www.axappphealth care.co.uk for all the international packages.

HEALTHCARE

As already mentioned, it is recommended that you secure private health insurance if you are going to move to Morocco as the health service is poor. Alternatively, you could simply 'pay as you go' and pay for treatment as and when you need it – however, it is generally safer simply to take out international health insurance. If you have a Carte de séjour, you are technically entitled to free state healthcare, although generally you will only get attention if you are prepared to pay.

The private clinics and hospitals in the country are mostly focused around Casablanca and the other big cities. There are more private doctors practising in the country than state-paid doctors, but many of the private practises are suffering a cash crisis given that the majority of the population cannot afford to pay for private treatment.

Pharmacies can be found everywhere in Morocco and they are certainly more lenient than in the UK, with customers allowed to order medicines over the counter. They can be identified from the outside by either the universal green cross symbol or a green crescent.

You will need vaccinations prior to leaving for Morocco, and the following are generally recommended for all travellers:

◆ Hepatitis A

◆ Typhoid

In certain circumstances you should have the following, or at least ensure you are up to date with them:

◆ Hepatitis B

◆ Rabies

◆ Measles, mumps, rubella (MMR)

◆ Tetanus-diphtheria

Consult your doctor for more information.

WORKING AND THE WORK ETHIC

The Western European work ethic is rather bewildering to the Moroccans. To them, life is centred around family and home life, believing that this, rather than your work and career, is what determines your lifestyle and routine – work just isn't seen as holding the same level of importance as in Europe. Western Europeans, by contrast, are the opposite as we often allow our jobs to dictate our lives. Consequently, you'll find that a Moroccan takes a rather relaxed approach to their work, although they are by no means work shy – it simply doesn't occupy such a central position in their life. Again, the influence of fatalism among much of the Moroccan population means the pursuit of career development is relatively unknown. It's seen only as a means of furthering the family's social position rather than achieving something on a personal level.

Many foreigners who come to Morocco do so for work reasons. There are fairly strict guidelines in place regarding work and work permits, and the jobs that foreign workers are allowed to take are restricted. This is due to the fact that the government pursues a policy whereby they would rather see a Moroccan given a job over a foreign worker and, unless a company can prove there is no local worker to fill the position, as a foreigner you are unlikely to be granted a work or residency permit.

Top tip

If you intend to work or set up a business in Morocco then it is essential that you speak French, or that you employ a friend or work with someone trustworthy who does. Knowing the language is the only way to navigate the bureaucracy that surrounds this process.

STARTING A BUSINESS IN MOROCCO

Morocco is rapidly developing as an economic powerhouse, and so investing and doing business here has the potential to be beneficial and profitable to all involved. With foreign investment strongly encouraged by the government, now is a great time to look at setting up your own business.

When applying to set up a business you must make it clear to the CRIs and ministeries involved that this will be a beneficial project for both Morocco and the Moroccan people, as well as yourself – i.e. that it will offer job opportunities to the local labour market and help to bring money into the country. In return the benefits are immense, with investment being encouraged through a simplified taxation process, transfer taxes slashed for property investors, and the amount of capital required to start a business cut from 100,000 dirhams to 10,000 dirhams.

The procedure is by no means straightforward, so be prepared for complicated bureaucracy and many hoops to jump through, while things will take longer than you would anticipate.

There are hundreds of different ways to set up a business in Morocco, each varying depending on your goals, the sector you intend to operate within and the duration of the business.

One of the first things to ascertain is the duration your business will last – essentially, will it be long or short term? Depending on the answer to this question you may or may not need to set up a legally registered company in order to carry out your business, which will also have repercussions on the payment of tax. Generally speaking, short-term agreements only require you to have a branch set up in Morocco rather than a legally registered company, yet tax will still be payable in Morocco, the country where the income has been generated.

You may be able to carry out your business transactions from outside the country without maintaining a presence there – for example, for research and development – and, again, this will have tax implications.

Depending on your business type, you may be setting up as an individual or as a company. If you want to set up a company, you have the choice of a limited or public company. Alternatively, you may remain outside Morocco and work with a dependant agent who is solely employed by you which will see you deemed as having a permanent establishment within the country and consequently liable to pay tax.

If you intend to open a hospital, bank, airline carrier or other credit institution then you will also have to approach the relevant government ministry and follow their business regulations.

Clearly there are many variables when looking to set up a business in Morocco, and these all depend on the type of business you want to run and your individual circumstances. Always ensure you take legal and business advice in order to get things done properly.

Useful contacts:

◆ Landwell & Associés: 219, Boulevard Zerktouni, Casablanca Anfa 20 100, Tel: +212 22 95 38 8, www.landwell.fr

◆ British Chamber of Commerce: www.bccm.co.ma

◆ British Embassy in Morocco: www.britishembassy.gov.uk/morocco

BENEFITS AND SOCIAL SECURITY PAYMENTS

If you are employed in Morocco, or you're a resident in the country and have applied for a Carte de séjour, you are entitled to free healthcare and education. You will also be required to pay some social security contributions if working in the country, which varies from 3.96% to 7.93% of your gross monthly income. To find out more, visit www.cnss.ma.

If you are looking to retire to Morocco and wish to continue claiming your state pension, then you can arrange for it to be paid into your bank account. However, as Morocco is currently outside the European Economic Area (EEA), your pension would no longer be index linked and would be frozen at the amount you receive when leaving the country, instead of rising in line with inflation.

Your state pension can be paid directly into a UK bank or building society account (or an EU account) but not into a bank in Morocco. Alternatively, you could have a sterling cheque sent to either your home address in Morocco or to your bank in Morocco, with the money then being converted into the local currency. If you divide your time between the UK and Morocco, you'll have to choose which country you want to receive your state pension in as you can't receive a cheque in Morocco for six months, for example, and then in the UK for the rest of the year.

As to whether or not you will pay tax on your pension in Morocco or your home country, this will depend on whether you're classed as a UK resident or a resident in Morocco for tax purposes. If you spend part of your time in the UK and part abroad you're likely to be classed as a UK resident. If you move to Morocco permanently, you'll be classed as a non-UK resident, so you're more likely to have to pay tax on your pension in Morocco. However, due to the double taxation treaty which is in place between the two countries you won't be taxed twice. To find out more, contact HM Revenue and Customs Centre for Non-Residents (www.hmrc.gov.uk).

As Morocco is outside of the EEA, any benefits you currently receive within the UK will be non-exportable to Morocco – in other words you won't be able to receive them. It is only recently that certain benefits have been payable to some EU countries.

If you're moving to Morocco, you'll need to inform the following organisations and give them your change of address:

◆ The Pension Service (www.thepensionservice.gov.uk)

◆ HM Revenue & Customs National Insurance Contributions Office (www.hmrc.gov.uk)

◆ Your Tax Office

RETIREMENT

Morocco has long been a popular location for French retirees, many of whom are based in Rabat and Casablanca. Morocco has a lot to offer retirees, from the wonderful climate to the miles of coastline and many cultural diversions. However, many people who choose to retire in Morocco have lived and worked there for many years, and know the country well. If you have never lived there, you should get to know Morocco well before upping sticks and relocating– it is a very different experience from Western Europe, and not all people of retirement age are guaranteed to adjust well.

In terms of legality, securing residency in Morocco is fairly straightforward, although it can take time. You will be entitled to stay in the country for three months on your passport, but if you intend to stay permanently, after 15 days in Morocco you will need to go to your local police station and apply for a residency permit. For more details, see Chapter 9.

EDUCATION

One fifth of the Moroccan budget is spent on education but most of this goes on school buildings rather than teaching. Education is mandatory for children between 7 and 13 years of age, with three quarters of school-age boys attending, but only half of school-age girls. There are low levels of attendance among rural communities, with Morocco's literacy level at 52.3% of the total population compared with 99% in the UK. Just over half of over-15s go on to pursue secondary education, with few seeking further education – Morocco only has four universities in the whole country.

Generally speaking the state education system is poor, with only the working classes sending their children there. Middle-class Moroccans tend to send their children to French-speaking private schools, while the wealthy educate their children overseas, generally in Europe. While the state system is free, resources are limited and teaching is in Arabic.

The only English-speaking schools in the country are the handful of international institutions that are located in Morocco's larger cities, and all are independents that teach children aged from 3 to 18. There are also a number of French-speaking schools, or private schools, and these are found throughout the country and follow a similar structure to the UK primary and secondary education system. Most pupils that attend these schools are Moroccan.

Generally speaking, you should send your child to an independent school, unless you plan to stay in Morocco long-term and want them to learn Arabic – but even then, the standard of education is much higher in a private establishment than in a state school.

Useful contacts

English-language schools

Casablanca American School
Route de La Mecque, Lotissement Ougoug, Quartier Californie, Casablanca 20150
+212 (0) 22 21 41 15
www.cas.ac.ma

George Washington Academy
Km 5.6 Rte d'Azemmour, Dar Bouazza, Casablanca 20220
+212 (0) 22 95 30 00
www.gwa.ac.ma

The American School of Tangier
149, Rue Christophe Colombe, Tangier 90000
+212 (0) 39 93 98 27
www.as-t.org

The American School of Marrakesh
Km 10 Rue d'Ouarzazate, Marrakesh 40000
+212 (0) 44 32 98 61
http://asm.ma

Rabat American School
1 Bis Rue Emir Ibn Abdelkader, Agdal, Rabat 10000
+212 37 671 476
www.ras.edu.ac.ma

Amicitia American School Fès
68 Avenue Allah Ben Abdellah, Fès 30000
+212 (0) 35 65 01 26
www.americanschoolfes.com

English-language university

Al Akhawayn University
PO Box 104 Hassan II Avenue, Ifrane 53000
+212 (0) 35 86 20 00
www.aui.ma

List of French-language schools in Morocco

www.ambafrance-ma.org/efmaroc/moliere/Mpages/liens.htm#sites
decoles

General contacts

www.britishcouncil.org/morocco
www.ambafrance-ma.org

DRIVING AND BUYING A CAR

Generally Moroccans drive sensibly, although some taxi drivers can be dangerous, with Casablanca being a hotspot for poor drivers. Roads are of good quality and many new highways are being built. However, provincial road standards vary. Be aware that there is a strong police presence in the country so ensure you keep to the speed limit as regular checks take place. Remember that Moroccans drive on the right-hand side of the road, with speed limits varying from 40 km per hour in the cities to 60–80 km per hour on the bigger roads and 120 km per hour on the highways. In Morocco it is compulsory to wear your seatbelt – both drivers and passengers, in the front and back of the car – and you must also always have your car headlights switched on.

There are many roadside petrol stations, although prices can – amazingly – be even higher than in the UK.

As import tax on international cars is very high, it can be more cost effective to buy a car once you have relocated. It is relatively quick and easy to buy a car in Morocco and there are many second-hand models available, especially from expats who may be returning to their home country. For example, a three-year-old Honda CR-V would set you back £5,500. New car prices are similar to those overseas. However, you can find cheaper deals, so take a look at some expat forums for ideas of where to buy and also to see if anyone is selling. The easiest way to buy is to pay cash.

GETTING AROUND

Bus

Every major Moroccan destination is served by bus, and this is the cheapest and most efficient way to travel around the country. However, be aware that conditions vary greatly with some services offering limited legroom and no air conditioning for long journeys. As such, it is often better to travel by night during the hot months. Generally speaking, you will be charged around 5 dirhams for baggage handling, with tickets costing between 70 dirhams and 150 dirhams depending on where you are going, the standards of travel and whether you choose to go first or second class.

There are a mix of private and national operators, with the main one being Compagnie de Transports Morocains (CTM, www.ctm.co.ma) which is based in Casablanca. It offers services throughout Morocco and into Europe and its buses are modern, with both heating and air conditioning available. Also recommended, and travelling throughout Morocco, is Supratours (www.supratours.ma) and SATAS, although some travellers have reported that SATAS doesn't enjoy a great reputation. There are also a number of smaller operators but some of these have very iffy travelling conditions, so be prepared. Local buses are also in operation, but only in larger cities such as Casablanca and Marrakesh; tickets generally cost around 3 dirhams.

Train

Morocco's rail network is far from comprehensive, with some popular destinations such as Essaouira and Agadir not served at all. That said, Morocco offers Africa's best rail service with cheap fares, regular trains and no need to pre-book. The main line connects Tangier, Meknès, Fès, Oujda, Rabat, Casablanca and Marrakesh, and you can find out more about fares and timetables from the Office National des Chemins de Fer, Morocco's national rail operators (www.oncf.ma). There are also overnight services in operation.

Air

You can purchase internal flights in Morocco, although they are expensive and there are only two operators at present: Air Maroc (www.royalairmaroc.com) and the more business orientated Regional Air Lines (www.regionalmaroc.com), which also tends to be more expensive. There are daily flights in operation from Casablanca to Tangiers, Marrakesh and Agadir.

Taxis

In Morocco, a system of Grand Taxis and Petit Taxis is in operation. Both are multiple hire, rather than the private system we operate in the UK, and there is the option of fixed-rate fares as well as meters. Petit Taxis are restricted to operating within the city limits while Grand Taxis link neighbouring towns together. Be aware that Grand Taxi drivers have a bit of a bad reputation as dangerous drivers who work long shifts with little sleep.

LEARNING THE LANGUAGE

If you intend to move to or buy in Morocco, it is recommended that you learn the language – probably French – in order to help you settle in the country. While English is being introduced at school level, French is much more widely spoken as it is country's unofficial second language. It is taught in schools (although it may seem slightly different from your school learnt French), and it's the language of commerce and business. Spanish is also spoken in the north, although only in pockets and not as widespread as French. There are also three Berber dialects, although it is unlikely that you will ever need to master these.

Arabic is the official Moroccan language and it is difficult to get the hang of, being a different dialect to normal Arabic. However, by learning a few key words and phrases you will gain the respect of the locals, and you'll also find that you pick up a lot more of the language along the way. If you want to learn Arabic, contact the English-language university in Fès about courses (Al Akhawayn University, www.aui.ma) or the Arabic Language Institute in Fès (www.alif-fes.com). Alternatively, there are many English-based language schools who are happy to arrange placements in Morocco. One of these is Cesa Languages (www.cesalanguages.com).

Did you know?
Unlike the French, Moroccans tend to say 'tu', rather than 'vous'.

SHOPPING

Morocco is a shopaholic's dream. From the souks of the medinas to the workshops of the traditional artisans and the shopping centres of the modern cities, your credit card will take a battering. Morocco is world-renowned for its arts and crafts, being home to some of the world's finest artisans who can recreate traditional ironwork and woodcarvings for your Moroccan home.

Carpets are ubiquitous in Morocco, from the Islamic-style rugs found in Rabat to the more locally styled Berber carpets of the Atlas ranges. Jewellery, wool and ceramics are also produced across the country, while Fès has a thriving leather-making district. Street vendors sell some of the world's finest snacks (see Chapter 1 on food and drink), while trinkets and souvenirs can be found at every turn – although beware the inferior-quality items that are produced just for foreigners. Moroccan souks are among the most colourful locations in the world, with everything from herbs and spices to textiles and brass, and are must-sees when in the country. Remember to barter though – bartering isn't offensive, it is simply part of the social culture of shopping, and you should generally try to reduce the price by one-third.

On a more mundane note, when buying everyday goods you'll be able to find some fabulous fresh fruit and vegetables at the local markets. Souks also provide everything from textiles, rugs and furniture to your weekly stock of herbs and spices, as well as meat and bread, making this the ideal place to get your supplies and furnishings.

Outside of the souks, a number of hypermarkets have grown up in the major conurbations, such as Marjane which includes mostly imported produce and is Morocco's largest hypermarket chain with 21 million customers. There is also Dutch company METRO AG Morocco (www.metrogroup.de) and Moroccan group Aswak As-salam. These hypermarkets may be handy but, thankfully, they're unlikely to replace the colourful souks, simply because over 40% of the population can't afford to shop in them or travel to them as they are normally located several kilometres outside of town.

Marjane locations

◆ Rabat (Bouregreg)

◆ Casablanca (Californie, Mers Sultan, Hay Hassani and Aïn Sebaâ)

◆ Marrakesh (Ménara)

◆ Rabat (Hay Riad)

◆ Agadir (Founty)

- Tanger (Madina)
- Fès (Agdal)
- Mohammedia
- Tétouan
- Meknès
- Marrakesh (Massira Sâada)
- Oujda Angad
- Safi (opened 2007)
- Kénitra (opening 2008)
- El Jadida (Hay Abdelilah echouhayri) (opening 2010)

POST

The Moroccan postal service is run by Poste Maroc (www.bam.net.ma), which offers many of the financial and courier services that UK post offices do. The postal service is good in Morocco – it's slow, but reliable – although you'll find that letters reach their destination faster if sent from larger cities. You'll be able to identify a Moroccan post office by the PTT or La Poste logo, and for small purchases, such as stamps, you can also visit tabacs (newsagents).

If you want to send a parcel overseas, you'll have to take it to the post office unwrapped so it can be inspected by customs officers – just remember to bring your own packaging materials to save money. There is a 20kg limit on parcel weight and sending mail varies in price from 6 dirhams to 20 dirhams for internal letters, rising all the way up to 550 dirhams to send a parcel overseas.

CRIME

Morocco is generally a safe place in which to live, with little violent crime occurring – more thefts and robberies are committed here than anything else. As a foreigner you will be a target for pickpockets and petty theft, so be aware when travelling and keep you possessions safely hidden – store your cash in a money belt or hard-to-reach place.

Appendices

APPENDIX 1: DIRECTORY OF USEFUL CONTACTS

Air travel

Air Maroc
www.royalairmaroc.com

Regional Air Lines
www.regionalmaroc.com

Atlas Blue
www.atlas-blue.com

BA
www.ba.com

easyJet
www.easyjet.com

Ryanair
www.ryanair.com

Skyjet.co.uk
www.skyjet.co.uk

First Choice
www.firstchoice.co.uk

Thomas Cook
www.flythomascook.com

GB Airways
www.gbairways.com

Thomsonfly
www.thomsonfly.com

Currency exchange

Caxton FX
0845 658 2223
www.caxtonfx.com

Conti Financial Services
01273 772811
www.mortgagesoverseas.com

Baydon Hill
0871 0705555
www.baydonhill.com

Currencies Direct
0845 3893000
www.currenciesdirect.com

Escape Currency
08000 321 109
www.escapecurrency.com

Globex
0207 253 7183
www.globexfx.com

HIFX PLC
01753 859159
www.hifx.co.uk

Moneycorp
020 7589 3000
www.moneycorp.com

SGM FX
020 7220 1740
www.sgm-fx.com

Online currency exchange rates
www.xe.com

Embassies

American Embassy
2 Avenue de Mohamed El Fassi, Rabat 10000
+212 (0) 37 76 22 65
www.usembassy.ma

British Embassy in Morocco
28 Avenue S.A.R. Sidi Mohammed, Souissi, Rabat 10000
+212 (0) 37 63 33 33
generalenquiries.rabat@fco.gov.uk
www.britain.org.ma

Moroccan Embassy in London
49 Queens Gate Gardens London SW7 5NE
020 7581 5001
http://morocco.embassyhomepage.com

Estate agents

Compass Properties
+212 (0) 3999 1770
www.compasspropertiesabroad.com

Francophiles
01622 688165
http://morocco.francophiles.co.uk

GEM Estates
0800 731 8494
www.gemestates.co.uk

Moroccan Homes
www.moroccan-homes.com
+34 (0) 95 25 08 961

Moroccan Properties Immobilier
+212 (0) 24 430 465
www.moroccan-properties.com

Moroccan Properties Ltd
020 8572 2422
www.moroccanpropertiesltd.com

Moroccan Sands
0800 856 3005
www.moroccansands.com

Moroccan Venture
www.moroccanventure.co.uk

Prestige Properties Overseas
0800 085 1601
www.prestigepropertiesoverseas.com

Saffron Villas
01635 391150
www.saffronvillas-morocco.co.uk

Expat advice

www.expatfocus.com
www.expat-blog.com
www.expatnetwork.co.uk
www.internationalliving.com
www.shelteroffshore.com
www.britishexpats.com
www.africaguide.com/forum/morocco

Government offices UK

Department of Health
020 7210 4850
www.dh.gov.uk

Department of Work and Pensions
Overseas pensions service: 0191 218 7777
www.dwp.gov.uk

Foreign and Commonwealth Office
Main switchboard: 020 7008 1500
Services for Britons overseas: 020 7008 0210
Travel advice: 0845 850 2829
Visa enquiries: 0845 010 5555
www.fco.gov.uk

Jobcentre Plus
www.jobcentreplus.gov.uk

Website of UK Government
www.direct.gov.uk

Government offices Morocco

British Embassy
28 Avenue S.A.R. Sidi Mohammed, Souissi, Rabat 10000
+212 (0) 37 63 33 33
www.britishembassy.gov.uk/morocco

British Council Morocco
36, Rue de Tanger, BP 427, Rabat 10000
+212 (0) 37 76 08 36
www.britishcouncil.org/morocco

Government of Morocco
Gouvernment du Royaume du Maroc, www.maroc.ma

Holiday lettings

www.holiday-rentals.co.uk
www.holidaylettings.co.uk
www.holidaylets.net

Insurance

AIG
020 7954 7000
www.aigeurope.co.uk

Allianz
01483 568161
www.allianz.com

Generali Worldwide Insurance Company Limited
01481 715 400
www.generali-gw.com

John Wason
0118 9568800
www.johnwason.co.uk

Investment
American Chamber of Commerce
www.amcham-morocco.com

British Chamber of Commerce
www.bccm.co.ma

CRI Agadir
www.cri-agadir.ma

CRI Casablanca
www.casainvest.ma

CRI Marrakesh
www.crimarrakech.ma

CRI Fes
www.crifes.ma

CRI Rabat
www.rabatinvest.ma

CRI Tangier
www.investangier.com

Direction des investissements extérieurs
www.invest-in-morocco.gov.ma

CRI du Grand Casablanca
www.casablanca.ma

Legal and financial

Baydon Hill
0871 0705555
www.baydonhill.com

Bennett & Co International Lawyers
0870 428 6177
www.bennett-and-co.com

Blevins Franks Financial Management
020 7336 114 / 020 7015 2158
www.blevinsfranks.com

International Mortgage Plans
01932 830660
www.international-mortgage-plans.com

JD Mortgages
01443 203111
www.jdmortgages.co.uk

The International Law Partnership
020 7061 6700 / 020 7061 6748
www.lawoverseas.com

The International Property Law Centre (part of The Max Gold Partnership Solicitors)

0870 800 4565
www.internationalpropertylaw.com

Landwell & Associés
219 Boulevard Zerktouni, Casablanca Anfa 20100
+212 (0) 22 95 38 8
www.landwell.fr

Motoring

Drive Safe
www.nationalcar.co.uk

AA Route Planner
www.theaa.com/travelwatch/planner_main.jsp

News

www.magharebia.com

Maghreb Arabe Presse
www.map.ma/eng

Gouvernment du Royaume du Maroc
www.maroc.ma

List of Moroccan Newspapers and News sites
www.world-newspapers.com/morocco.html

Removals

1st Move International Removals
0117 9828123
www.shipit.co.uk

Allied Pickfords
0800 289 229
http://gb.allied.com

Anglo Pacific
0800 7834418
www.anglo-pacific.co.uk

Britannia
0800 622 535
www.britannia-movers.co.uk

European Removals
0800 980 5867
www.europeanremovals.com

F + N International Removals
0800 583 4844 / 01476 579210
www.fnworldwide.com

International Removals
0800 783 1085 / 020 8324 2066
www.international-removals.com

Relocation Enterprises
+39 06 82 40 60
www.relocationenterprises.com

Robinsons
01235 552266
www.robinsons-intl.com

Telephone and internet

Listings of worldwide electrical and telephone information
www.kropla.com

Maroc Telecom
www.onpt.net.ma

Meditel
www.meditel.ma

Tax

Worldwide Tax
www.worldwide-tax.com

Blevins Franks Financial Management
020 7336 114/ 020 7015 2158
www.blevinsfranks.com

The International Property Law Centre (part of The Max Gold
Partnership Solicitors)
0870 800 4565
www.internationalpropertylaw.com

Landwell & Associés
219 Boulevard Zerktouni, Casablanca Anfa 20100
+212 (0) 22 95 38 8
www.landwell.fr

Travel and transport

Bus

Compagnie de Transports Morocains (CTM)
www.ctm.co.ma

Supratours
www.supratours.ma

Train

National Rail Service
www.oncf.ma

Internal flights

Air Maroc
www.royalairmaroc.com

Regional Air Lines
www.regionalmaroc.com

General links for Morocco

Business and Tourism Portal
www.1stmaroc.com

Tourist Office Morocco
www.visitmorocco.org

Travel, hotels and tourism
www.morocco.com

About Morocco
www.maroc-insight.com
http://en.wikipedia.org/wiki/List_of_Morocco-related_topics
http://en.wikipedia.org/wiki/Morocco
www.morocco-uk.com

APPENDIX 2: MOROCCAN PROPERTY MATRIX

Region	Typical properties and prices	Why invest?	Who buys here?	Hotspots
Chaouia-Ouardigha	There is limited property stock here in terms of estate agent coverage, but you can buy eight hectares of land for 300,000 dh	There has been new investment into the area and the market is very immature, with low prices	This is a local market with few foreigners investing	Benslimane, Settat
Doukkala-Abda	Prices range from £10,000 for a medina property to £50,000 for a new apartment to £65,000 within the Plan Azur resort of Mazagan	The areas of Azemmour and El Jadida are earmarked for development under Plan Azur. These are also stunning beachfront locations with affordable housing and many cultural attractions	There is a strong local presence thanks to Moroccan second-home buyers, although this is also popular for holiday homes, with great investment opportunities within the Plan Azur resorts	Safi, El Jadida, Oualidia, Azemmour

Fès-Boulemane	Prices in Fès start from £20,000 rising to around £170,000 for a large riad, and around £40,000 for a modern apartment	Fès is a cultural hotspot and offers a good standard of living, low property prices and some characterful properties, while Sefrou, being off the tourist trail, is cheap and in countryside surroundings	Investors looking for good rental income and increasing numbers of holiday-home buyers	Fès, Sefrou
Gharb-Chrarda-Béni Hssen	With few traditional properties, you are looking at £48,000 for a modern two-bedroom apartment	If you're looking for a local area that's unspoilt then this is it. House prices are cheap too	Mostly locals	Kenitra
Greater Casablanca	Prices vary drastically, ranging from £70,000 to £500,000+	Cosmopolitan and lively, this is an up-and-coming hotspot with major investment being carried out	Good for investors	Casablanca

Region	Typical properties and prices	Why invest?	Who buys here?	Hotspots
Guelmim-Es Semara	The Plage Blanche development is set to offer homes from roughly £50,000, while Guelmim has land for as little as £5,500 for 110 sq m	Earmarked for development, this region offers miles of sandy coastline and low property prices. Isolated at present but up-and-coming	A future investment location but currently a local market	Tan Tan, Plage Blanche, Guelmim
Laâyoune-Boujdour-Sakia El Hamra	Thanks to government investment in Laâyoune, there are many modern if uninspiring homes here, as well as plots of land. Outside of the city, homes are generally in the form of simple fisherman's huts	The government is offering very cheap land prices as an incentive to buy here	Investors perhaps, but in truth there is little movement in the market	Laâyoune
Marrakesh-Tensift-El Haouz	Riads range from £50,000 to £300,000, and from £30,000 to £100,000 in Essaouira	This is the hottest market in Morocco, and it's also the most developed and in-demand, with massive potential and huge investment	Investors, retirees and holiday-home buyers	Marrakesh, Essaouira

Meknès-Tafilalet	A 12-bedroom riad in Meknès can be bought for £300,000, while for £280,000 you can buy a farm on the outskirts of the town. Newly built homes in Ifrane start from £30,000	Ifrane is set to be an up-and-coming ski resort and is very European in nature, while Meknès offers some cheap medina properties and is a well-located UNESCO World Heritage site	Few foreigners are buying here although the market is set to grow	Meknès, Ifrane
Oriental	In the Mediterranea Saïdia, prices range from £80,000 through to £300,000	This is one of the most popular locations on the Mediterranean Coast, with the Mediterrania Saïdia resort being a flagship Plan Azur development	Investors, second-home buyers and retirees	Saïdia , Oujda, Berkane, Nador
Oued Ed-Dahab-Lagouira		Land here is incredibly cheap	This is a very isolated place with a restricted market and no foreign interest	Dakhlaz
Rabat-Salé-Zemmour-Zaer	From £30,000 for a modern apartment to £250,000 for a villa	There is major investment and redevelopment taking place here, and the future looks bright for tourism and investment	Mainly investors, although it's also popular with French retirees	Rabat, Salé

Region	Typical properties and prices	Why invest?	Who buys here?	Hotspots
Souss-Massa-Draâ	Prices range from £50,000 rising to £350,000 in exclusive areas. A ruined fisherman's cottage can be found for £10,000	This is a major hotspot and a highly recommended market to look at, thanks to Plan Azur and the pristine beaches	Investors and second-home buyers	Agadir, Ouarzazate, Aglou Plage, Mirflet, Taghazoute
Tadla-Azilal		Lush and fertile, good for eco-tourism or activity holidays	Not on the foreign agenda, the market is fairly inactive	Beni Mellal
Tangier-Tétouan	From £50,000 to £70,000, rising to £150,000 in Tangier	This is a bustling area, popular with holiday-makers and earmarked for major redevelopment	Investors and second-home buyers	Tangier, Tetouan, Chefchaouen
Taza-Al Hoceima-Taounate	A farmhouse can be bought for £35,000 and a large house for £250,000	Quiet laid-back resorts and low prices	Foreign interest is minimal	Taza, Al Hoceima

APPENDIX 3: USEFUL INFORMATION

Public Holidays in 2008

1 January: New Year's Day
10 January: Fatih Muharram (Muslim New Year)
11 January: Manifeste de l'Indépendance (Manifesto of Independence)
20 March: Aïd al-Mawlid (Prophet's Birthday)
1 May: Labour Day
30 July: Fête du Trone (Feast of the Throne)
14 August: Fête Oued Eddahab (Oued Eddahab Allegiance Day)
20 August: Révolution du Roi et du Peuple (Anniversary of the King and the People's Revolution)
21 August: King Mohammed's Birthday
2 October: Aïd al-Fitr (End of Ramadan)
6 November: Marche Verte (Anniversary of the Green March)
18 November: Fête de l'Indépendance (Independence Day)
9 December: Aïd al-Adha (Feast of the Sacrifice)
29 December: Fatih Muharram (Muslim New Year)

Public Holidays in 2009

1 January: New Year's Day
11 January: Manifeste de l'Indépendance (Manifesto of Independence)
9 March: Aïd al-Mawlid (Prophet's Birthday)
1 May: Labour Day
30 July: Fête du Trone (Feast of the Throne)
14 August: Fête Oued Eddahab (Oued Eddahab Allegiance Day)
20 August: Révolution du Roi et du Peuple (Anniversary of the King and the People's Revolution)
21 August: King Mohammed's Birthday
21 September: Aïd al-Fitr (End of Ramadan)

6 November: Marche Verte (Anniversary of the Green March)
18 November: Fête de l'Indépendance (Independence Day)
28 November: Aïd al-Adha (Feast of the Sacrifice)

Dialling codes

Country code 00 212 (+212)

City dialling codes

Prefix with +212 if dialling from outside the country
Agadir: 8
Beni Mella: 348
Berrechid: 2
Casablanca: 22
El Jadida: 334
Kenitra: 73
Khouribga: 49
Marrakesh: 42
Meknès: 5
Mohammedia: 332
Nador: 660
Oujda: 562
Rabat: 7
Safi: 46
Salé: 380
Tanger: 99
Tetouan: 996

Emergency phone numbers

Police: 19
Ambulance: 15

Morocco postal codes

Agadir 80 000
Al Hoceima 32 000
Azilal 22 000
Ben Slimane 13 000
Beni Mellal 23 000
Boujdour 71 000
Boulemane 33 000
Casablanca 20 000
Chefchaouen 91 000
Chichaoua 41 000
Dakhla 73 000
El Jadida 24 000
Errachidia 52 000
Essaouira 44 000
Fès 30 000
Figuig 61 000
Guelmim 81 000
Ifrane 53 000
Kelaa des Sraghna 43 000
Kénitra 14 000
Khemisset 15 000
Khenifra 54 000
Khouribga 25 000
Laâyoune 70 000

Larache 92 000
Marrakesh 40 000
Meknès 50 000
Mohammedia 20 650
Nador 62 000
Ouarzazate 45 000
Oujda 60 000
Rabat 10 000
Safi 46 000
Salé 11 000
Sefrou 31 000
Settat 26 000
Sidi Kacem 16 000
Smara 72 000
Tangier 90 000
Tan-Tan 82 000
Taounate 34 000
Taroudannt 83 000
Tata 84 000
Taza 35 000
Témara 12 000
Tetouan 93 000
Tiznit 85 000

APPENDIX 4: GLOSSARY AND USEFUL PHRASES

Arabic

adhan: the call to prayer
agdal: garden or park containing a pool
aguelmane: lake
arabesque: geometrical decoration or calligraphy

bab: gate or door
babouches: slippers
bali (qdim): old
bled: countryside/land
bordj: fort

caid: district administrator

dar: house or palace
daya/deyet: lake
djebel: mountain peak or ridge
djedid/jdid: new
djemaa/jamaa: mosque, or Friday which is the main day of worship
djinn: spirit or genie

Fassi: inhabitant of Fès

hadj: pilgrimage to Mecca
hammam: Turkish-style steam bath

Imam: prayer leader and elder of a mosque

kasbah: palace centre and/or fortress of an Arab town; also used to
    mean a walled residential quarter around the Medina or citadel
ksar/ksour: southern village or tribal stronghold

maghreb: this means 'west' in Arabic and refers to the Moroccan
    and north African countries
makhzen: government
medina: city, although in modern usage it refers to the original Arab
    part of any Moroccan town

mellah: Jewish quarter
minaret: tower attached to a mosque, used for call to prayer
mouloud: festival and birthday of the Prophet
moussem: pilgrimage-festival
msalla: prayer area
muezzin/mueddin: singer who calls the faithful to prayer

piste: unsurfaced road or track

ramadan: month of fasting
ras el ma: water source
riad: a house built around a central courtyard with a garden
ribat: monastic fortress

Sheikh: leader of religious brotherhood
Shreef: descendant of the Prophet
Sidi/Si: respectful title used for any man, e.g. Sir, Mr
souk: market, or market quarter

tabia/pisé: mud building material

zellij: geometrical mosaic tilework

Useful phrases

Hello: Salaam alaikum
Goodbye: Baslamma
How are you?: Labass?
Fine, thank you: Alhamdulillah
Thank you: Choukran
I am sorry: Smahali
Nice to meet you: Misharafin
God willing: Insh'Allah
Mr/Sir: Saïd
Mrs/Madam: Saïda
Miss: Anissa

Do you speak English?: Ouesh tat tkelem belinglisia blin-gliz?
How much is it?: Besh hal hada?
It is expensive: Ghaliya

Where is . . .?: Fein . . .?
I need a room: Bghit bit
I want to buy: Bghit nechr
I don't know: Ma naarafsh
I don't understand: Ma fahemtsh
I am lost: Ana mouaddar

airport: lmatar
train station: mahatat al ketar
hotel: al foundouk
restaurant: al mataam
bathroom: bit al ma
post office: al bosta
telephone: atilifoon
pharmacy: pharmacien
bank: al banca
embassy: sifara

a little: shwiya
too much: bzaaf
water: al'ma
bread: al'khobz
coffee: al kahoua
tea: atay
vegetables: al khoudra
I need: Bghit

French

acquérir: to buy
Acte de vente: final contract of sale
agence: agency
agrandissement: extension
alimentation: supply (water, electricity, etc.)
aménager: to convert
à rénover: to renovate
à restaurer: to restore

balcon: balcony
banque: bank
bois: wood
boiserie: woodwork
bon état: good condition
bord de mer: by the sea
bureau: office

Carte de séjour: residency permit
campagne: countryside
chambre: bedroom
chantier: building site
chaudière: water heater
chauffage: heating
chauffage central: central heating
chauffe eau: hot water tank
commodités: lavatory
climatisation: air conditioning
cuisine: kitchen

dallage: paving
dalle: flag stone
débarras: box room
décapant: paint stripper
décorée: decorated
douche: shower
démenagement: moving house
délabré: dilapidated

échafaudage: scaffolding
échelle: ladder
éclairage: lighting
équipé: equipped
escabeau: step ladder
escalier: stair
espace: space

fer: iron

ferme: farm
ferraillage: ironwork
fosse septique: septic tank
four: oven

location: rental
logement: accommodation
lingerie: washing room

maçon: builder
maison de campagne: country house
meubles: furniture
moquette: carpet
mortier: mortar
mortier colle: tile cement
moulure: moulding
mur: wall

neuf: new
notaire: notary

pièce: room
pierre: stone
plâtre: plaster
plomberie: plumbing
prise: electric socket
propriétaire: owner
propriété: property

refait: restored
rénové: renovated
réservoir: cistern
restauré: renovated
retraite: retirement place
revêtement: surface

salle de bains: bathroom
salon: living room
séjour: living room

sol: ground
sous-sol: underground, or basement

tapis: carpet
terrain: grounds, or plot of land
terre cuite: terracotta
toit/toiture: roof

vitre: glass
vue: view

Useful phrases

Do you speak English?: Parlez vous anglais?
Excuse me: Excusez moi
Good bye: Au revoir
Good evening: Bonsoir
Hello: Bonjour
What is your name?: Comment vous appellez-vous?
My name is . . .: Je m'appelle . . .
How are you?: Comment allez vous?
How is everything?: Comment ça va?
Help me please: Aidez moi s'il vous plaît
How do you get to . . .?: Comment fait on pour aller à . . .?
How long does it take to get there?: Ça prend combien de temps pour y aller?
How much is it?: Ça coûte combien?
I don't know how to say it in French: Je ne sais pas le dire en français
I don't speak French: Je ne parle pas français
I don't understand: Je ne comprends pas
Is this the right bus for . . .?: C'est bien l'autobus pour . . .?
Nice to meet you: Enchanté
See you tomorrow/soon: À demain/bientôt
Tasting: Dégustation
Thank you: Merci
Water is not for drinking: Eau non potable

Where are the toilets?: Où sont les toilettes?

Where is the nearest phone box?: Où se trouve la cabine téléphonique la plus proche?

Where is the nearest supermarket?: Où est le supermarché le plus près?

Yes/No: Oui/Non

You're welcome: Je vous en prie

Can I pay by credit card?: Puis-je payer avec une carte de credit?

Coins: Pièces

Do you accept credit cards?: Acceptez vous les cartes de crédit?

How much does it cost?: Combien ça coûte?/C'est combien?

Index